2020 Longhorn Football Prospectus: Thinking Texas Football

written by

Paul Wadlington

design by

Scott Gerlach

photography by

Will Gallagher

Print Edition

Print Edition, License Notes

Contents

Introduction

Greetings!

Welcome to the 8th annual *2020 Longhorn Football Prospectus: Thinking Texas Football.*

This book is a Texas football preview, a Big 12 season companion and reference guide, and a resource for the entire football season.

Thinking Texas Football, in deference to its name, is written for an intelligent football layperson. It won't insult you by writing down to the lowest common denominator nor will it try to overawe you with technical babble. The book's best ambition is to provide you with different tools - while plainly communicating an awareness of its own biases and blind spots - so that we can engage in a conversation that mutually enriches our shared passion.

If you like it, please write a review wherever you bought it and share it with your Longhorn network. This endeavor can't continue without your support.

Hook 'em!

* * * * *

The Predictable Unpredictable

Writing and independently publishing a season preview book that aspires to offer more depth, insight, and entertainment than the typical cookie cutter preview is a big task. It requires long hours of watching film, reviewing season notes, pouring through media guides, toppling lazy orthodoxies, delving into Longhorn history, and staying current on the latest intelligence in the college football world. You try to make sense of it all and then make a few predictions. Or preferably, provide a useful framework so that the reader can make their own. Making sound predictions in a time of viral lockdowns and renewed social activism, when campuses are fractured with tension, entire position groups could miss weeks of the season, or that season is delayed, is a challenge. Nonetheless, the insatiable appetite for college football, and its unique connection with state, school and past, a shared identity for those seeking community in a time of social isolation, and the desire to find a common ground where we can all come together, is powerful. If the uncertainty of the moment guarantees a constantly changing landscape, this book will do its best to lay out the most relevant factors and give you the tools to make your own adjustments on the fly.

Force majeure will have its say, but it always has.

Unfortunately, a disappointing 2019 Texas Longhorn football season was more attributable to the acts of man than a divine power. Unless you believe in Loki, god of mischief. Or Neglecto, god of forsaken instruction, negligent edge setting, and mindless blitz packages. Neglecto is a pretty specific deity.

Tom Herman agrees that the 2019 season was a disappointment. Proof of that agreement is that he fired 70% of his coaching staff after a 8-5 season replete with underperformance on the sidelines that showed up between the lines every Saturday. Gone are Tim Beck, Todd Orlando, Drew Mehringer, Corby Meekins, Craig Naivar, Derek Warehime, and Jason Washington. Some had hitched their wagons to the right horse, only to find themselves revealed by the Peter Principle, and others lost their way and forgot what coaching is really about. Some could coach, but found themselves crossed up by the larger environment. Assign the category as you see fit. Texas needed a drastic change. Short of firing Herman and starting over, a task that no one had the stomach for, this was the only way. Were those assistants just the fall guys of last Fall? We will know soon enough.

But some things are very predictable. When Tom Herman was hired after his terrific run at Houston and as an offensive coordinator at Ohio State, the 2017 preview book welcomed him and offered him a piece of advice. Well, actually a warning. It was this: All new Longhorn head coaches find out the hard way that the staff that was good enough to get them the Texas job will not be good enough for them to keep it. Transition is a time to upgrade, not double down. The failure to upgrade and explore the national market equipped with a Longhorn checkbook and resources to exploit the initiative afforded by the promise of untapped potential at an all-time elite program at the time of hire, is as predictable for new Longhorn head men as it is frustrating. It can be attributed to loyalty, an attribute we all value and respect, but in truth that loyalty is too often intertwined with the tendrils of hubris and parochialism. The leader can't see past his own limited network of contacts and experiences and conceives of himself as a bulletproof miracle worker. The proof? He just landed a Top 5 college job! Why did he land that job? Bulletproof miracle worker! We can all fall prey to that circularly reinforcing logic.

Was the staff that Tom Herman hired at the University of Houston and took largely intact to Texas the best one in the country? Was it even sufficient to excel on a bigger stage? We know that predictable answer now. In Herman's first year, the 2015 Houston Cougars went 13-1 against a schedule that featured Tennessee Tech, Texas State, Tulane, UConn, Vanderbilt, Tulsa, and SMU. At season's end, the 70th ranked strength of schedule in the nation. His 2016 team (9-3 record) had the 51st ranked strength of schedule. Houston is a potential kingmaking program (Pardee, Briles, Sumlin, Herman) with recruiting potential and football focus that outstrips their AAC peers. A head coach who succeeds there must understand that, anticipate the level up in competition that's coming in the new big job, and explore upgrades outside of his iPhone contacts.

It's true that hiring a staff is not an All-Star team - chemistry matters and coaches thrive on trust - but the most innovative coordinators, the best position teachers, the elite recruiting prodigies are well known (or knowable) in the high school, college, and NFL ranks. Kick some tires and see who you click with. At the same time, identifying and developing young up and comers, who bring essential energy and ambition into the building, is its own skill set. Some coaches do it brilliantly and profit, creating a legacy, and a coaching tree, that extends for generations. Others hire sycophants to serve as an affirming mini-Me.

The shortcomings of the 2019 Longhorn staff will be recounted in these pages in graphic detail that may threaten to make you as world weary and nihilistic as fellow Longhorn Matthew McConaughey's brilliant portrayal of Rust Cohle in *True Detective*, but for now we will stick to the big picture. A program that badly needed player development failed to do it. A program that needed only to operate at game-planning parity with its less talented conference peers failed to do it. Worst of all, the staff did not connect sufficiently with their pupils.

Many of the players felt that they were not in a meritocracy, despite lip service to the contrary. The evidence for their claim? The coaching ability of the men telling them it was a meritocracy. They saw players they had dominated in high school beating them on college fields and they began to wonder why. They saw an inability to equip them with the fundamental tools that they needed to get better. Players will put up with hard coaching and a high level of program control when they see their skills progress and wins start to stack up. Players will put up with far less when they know that they are stagnating and mired in mediocrity. Throw in the national expectations at a storied program, the player's own distorted self-perception fostered by recruiting rankings, add a dash of Texas is Back nonsense, and the stew of cognitive dissonance burns at a slow simmer.

That was the recipe for underachievement in the third year of Herman's regime - a time when the trend line should be pointing up, not leveling off. Tom Herman's postseason staff house cleaning implies agreement, even if he might bristle at the descriptions above and point to injuries, bad bounces, Charlie Strong's inheritance, or simple bad luck. The only necessary response to that is a shrug and a nod to the seven new faces in the staff room. It is not a perfect staff, but the predominant positive characteristic that it possesses is the ability to teach. It would be nice to enter the head coach's 4th year with this current staff having laid the foundations of the program at his time of hire. Texas might already have a Big 12 title or two in its pocket and a sense of tangible momentum. But there is no time like the present to tackle that mounting To Do list. First, the offense.

Offensive Overview

Let's examine the Texas OFEI (Offensive Fremeau Efficiency Index) offensive rankings since 2010. FEI is a useful advanced metric that adjusts for opponent strength, and factors in measures like starting field position, garbage time, and efficiency per drive. It calculates the per possession scoring advantage a team's offense would be expected to have on a neutral field against an average defense and also calculates drive efficiency by touchdowns, turnovers, 3 and outs, and explosive plays, to provide a deeper dive than a simple yards per game average. Ranked out of 130 FBS programs, here is how Texas has fared since 2010.

Year	Offensive Rank	Coordinator	Record
2010	101	Greg Davis	5-7
2011	59	Bryan Harsin	8-5
2012	14	Bryan Harsin	9-4
2013	62	Major Applewhite	8-5
2014	105	Shawn Watson	6-7
2015	93	Jay Norvell	5-7
2016	69	Sterlin Gilbert	5-7
2017	109	Tim Beck	7-6
2018	25	Tim Beck	10-4
2019	13	Tim Beck	8-5
2020		Mike Yurick	

Since 2010, the Texas offense has had eight offensive coordinators. Not ideal. Before Herman's arrival, the Longhorn offense averaged a 72nd national FEI ranking. Save the bright spot of Bryan Harsin's second (and last) season, that's hard to get your head around. Four seasons featuring an offensive FEI ranked 93rd or worse is not a powerful endorsement for Mike Yurcich's predecessors. If you want to truly understand Longhorn mediocrity over the past decade, take a hard look at the offensive side of the football.

During his three-year tenure, Herman improved Texas to a 49.0 average ranking and fielded back-to-back Top 25 offenses after an understandably rough debut in 2017. Jumping 84 spots in the rankings from 2017 to 2018 was extraordinarily encouraging as was an upward push into 2019, but if those trends are so favorable, why does Texas have a new offensive coordinator and a head coach vowing to take a step back from play-calling and game-planning? Because Tim Beck was the offensive coordinator in name only.

The deeper answer is rooted in game context, poor gameplanning, and high-profile failures against the quality conference defenses that know Texas best. The Texas offensive staff did a fine job in the first few games of the season letting talent win out, but as film compiled on both Texas and their opponents, issues around scouting and game planning came to a head. The Texas defense certainly disappointed consistently, but take a closer, more critical look at offensive performance in the four games that Texas dropped in conference play.

The offensive wheels first came off of the wagon in Dallas against Oklahoma. A 34-27 loss does not adequately reflect the schematic spanking that Oklahoma defensive coordinator Alex Grinch delivered to the Texas coaches, who were unprepared for anything Oklahoma's defense brought to the table. This was not about a Sooner wrinkle catching Texas flat-footed. Oklahoma's stunting defensive line, Neville Gallimore's bull rush, Kenneth Murray's interior blitzes, and the Sooners' clutching, grabbing, interference heavy man-to-man press coverage were well-documented coming into the game. It was all over Oklahoma's game film and Grinch's entire history as a defensive coordinator. The Longhorns surrendered an incredible 15 tackles for loss, nine sacks, and gained only 310 yards of offense. Never has a one touchdown loss felt more like a beating. It was a dispiriting effort by the Longhorn offensive brain trust.

Two weeks later, another trip to the Dallas-Fort Worth metro proved unsatisfying against the TCU Horned Frogs. A bad TCU team took down Texas, forcing Sam Ehlinger into four turnovers (in fairness, two were on Texas receivers). TCU scored 13 points off of Longhorn turnovers, gaining only 70 combined yards on those three drives. The Horns put up a seemingly respectable 27 points in the loss, but a stale second half Texas offense struggled after Gary Patterson made some basic halftime adjustments against the Longhorn passing game, which included benching a couple of Frogs defenders who weren't doing what he wanted. Ehlinger averaged 9.2 yards per passing attempt in the first half. In the second half, he averaged a woeful 4.4 yards per passing attempt as the Frogs broke up six passes and stole three interceptions. Unlike Oklahoma, TCU could not get consistent pressure up front - so they simply opted to cover, squatting down on simplistic route combinations, completely bottling Texas up in the second half. Texas had no countermeasures to Patterson's halftime adjustments. It was a slothful performance against a Frog team that would win only two more games in Big 12 play.

On the road in Ames, Tom Herman and the offensive staff laid another egg. Incapable of running the ball (Longhorn running backs combined for 27 yards on 14 carries) against Iowa State's physical front and opportunistically walked up safeties, Texas amassed only 327 yards and 21 points in a two-point loss. Texas went three and out on 61.5% - 8 of 13 - offensive possessions. Add in a pair of six and outs (the offense achieves one first down, then punts) and Texas was totally ineffective on 10 of its 13 offensive possessions. The beleaguered Texas defense deserves a nod for keeping it close. The instructive part that is too easily forgotten? Texas had three touchdown drives of 75, 80, and 89 yards, predominantly running four wide from spread tempo, throwing the football on nearly every down. The first touchdown drive came running hurry-up in the final possession of the first half. That 75-yard scoring drive took all of five plays and 30 seconds. It also prevented the Longhorns from being blanked in the first stanza. One would hope its success would suggest a course of action for the second half.

No such luck. The Horns gained 4 yards on 9 plays on their first three possessions out of halftime. The Longhorns trailed 20-7. Desperate, they went full Air Horn in the late 3rd quarter and asked Sam to get it done. Ehlinger was happy to comply with that late request. Texas threw on every down of a 10 play, 80-yard touchdown drive that took less than three minutes. 20-14, Iowa State.

Texas got the ball again, trailing by six on its 11-yard line, now midway through the 4th quarter. Ehlinger threw or ran for every positive gain on the drive. He also converted a 2nd and 35 with consecutive throws of 30 and 26 yards to Eagles and Duvernay, respectively. In all, Ehlinger engineered a brilliant 15 play, 89-yard touchdown drive with four third or fourth down conversions. 21-20, Texas. The Horns were cooking with gas and Iowa State's relative defensive weaknesses coming into the game - poor pass rush, lack of depth, two weak links in the secondary - were finally being exploited by an aggressive Longhorn offense. Those successful drives were nothing more than a box count, Sam Ehlinger with the ball in his hands, and frequent use of tempo so the Cyclones could not substitute or adjust. Whenever Sam saw a three-man rush, he held the ball patiently. Whenever he saw blitz or double teams outside, he dumped it to a back or took off running. Sometimes football is that simple. The Longhorn staff stubbornly saw it otherwise on ten other fruitless possessions. But the worst decision was yet to come.

The Horns held a 21-20 lead with 4:01 left in the game and, after a nice defensive effort, possessed the ball. Fresh off of consecutive long touchdown drives with Ehlinger throwing the ball in rhythm and running from the pocket. What happened next threatened the health of thousands of Longhorn television sets the world over. Tom Herman called two give up runs totaling zero yards and then threw a screen to Duvernay on 3rd down that was broken up by an Iowa State defensive tackle. Precisely the kinds of calls a head coach makes when he lacks confidence in an unreliable freshman quarterback, not a veteran signal caller who had just given Texas the lead with consecutive brilliant drives.

Beyond the inability to see the game as it was, or the betrayal of confidence in his best player, Herman did not understand the basic probability proposition that one cannot attack four minutes of clock without first attacking the chains. An offense cannot run out the clock with 4:01 on the board, particularly in the college game. Because...math. Don't forget that Texas runners were also averaging 1.9 yards per carry. You let the play clock run down, run the offense that has worked, prioritize gaining yardage above all, and force Iowa State to burn their timeouts as the offense keeps getting fresh downs. If you score again, even better. Texas burned all of one minute and one second "playing it safe" and Iowa State took over with plenty of time and a timeout reserved for the game winning field goal. Naturally, the Cyclones took the ball down the field for that game winning field goal, appropriately converted by a player named Assalley. A

well-deserved loss for an offensive staff that had exposed their alley all night.

The last straw was an anticlimactic loss to Baylor. That Tom Herman and Matt Rhule both began at their respective programs at the same time in the same league separated by 100 miles of I-35 pavement is useful information. Rhule was the appropriate control for the Herman program building experiment. Particularly when one acknowledges that Rhule swam against more brutal currents post-Briles than even Herman's weak Strong inheritance. Matt Rhule went 1-11 in his first year, but patiently rebuilt his team with sound coaching and development. The 2019 Bears defense was evidence of that fact. They controlled Texas from whistle to whistle. The first five Texas possessions of the game were punts. Baylor notched five sacks, two of them coming against Texas protection calls that had true freshman tight end

Jared Wiley attempting to block 290 pound Big 12 Defensive Player of the Year James Lynch. After being kept out of the end zone for four quarters, Texas made the score 24-10 on a Daniel Young touchdown plunge with :01 left on the clock. Texas ran the ball effectively at times, including a zippy 68-yard run from Keaontay Ingram, but the Bears jumped all over a predictable Texas passing game, sitting on route after formulaic route. The Texas offense simply had no juice.

Texas lost five games in 2019. In four of those losses, the offense was suboptimal, not coincidentally, against the four best defenses in the Big 12. The Longhorns averaged only 21.3 points per game, 368.8 yards, and an anemic 5.1 yards per play against those four opponents. Texas offensively bullied the remainder of their schedule, putting up plenty of points and yards against nine other opponents averaging 41.4 points per game, 509.9 yards per game, 6.9 yards per play. At the macro level, it's odd to be critical of an offense that averaged 35.2 points per game and 465.8 yards per contest at 6.4 yards per play. But if you were only interested in the easy, casual perspective, you would not have bought this prospectus. The top half of Big 12 defenses outcoached and outplayed the Texas offense while the Horns pummeled the league's worst.

Texas offense should not decline from dominating to disappointing simply because they encounter a defense with a strong pulse. Fireworks against Louisiana Tech,

Kansas, Texas Tech, and yes, LSU, yielded strong offensive numbers and fostered favorable advanced metrics rankings, but when you look under the hood of that stylish car, you find a low horsepower engine that could not handle steep hills or the curves that other staffs threw into the road. It should also be acknowledged that Texas was fortunate to have seen the Bayou Bengal defense in early September and not January. That Tiger defense grew up from cub to maneater.

We should be pleased that Tom Herman had sufficient self-reflection (or self-preservation) to make an offensive change. Sometimes fear does the work of reason. Whether he has the follow-through to allow his new offensive coordinator to run the show is another matter. That decision will not be a calculated choice of intellect, but rather one reflective of ego and temperament. Are you humble enough to understand your limitations as a coach and the second and third order effects of trying to control the things that should be tasked to subordinates? New offensive coordinator Mike Yurcich is at Texas to game plan each opponent, add fresh concepts, diversify the offense, and place more offensive control in the hands of a very good, very smart Texas quarterback. If that does not happen, and Texas continues to be outmatched on the headsets against the top half of the conference's defenses, the Longhorns are no longer experiencing a coordinator level issue.

Quarterback

11	Sam Ehlinger		6-2	230	Senior

Passing: 296/454-3663 YARDS, 32 TDS, 10 INT, 65.2% COMP | Rushing: 163-663 YARDS, 7 TDS, 4.1 YPC

8	Casey Thompson		6-0	190	Sophomore

Passing: 8/12-84 YARDS, 66.7% COMP | Rushing: 10-22 YARDS, 1 TDS, 2.2 YPC

1	Hudson Card		6-2	185	Freshman

	Ja'Quinden Jackson	6-2	220	Freshman

Before his senior season, **Sam Ehlinger** has already cemented himself as one of the best quarterbacks in Longhorn history. Over 33 starts and 36 game appearances, the senior quarterback has written his name at or near the top of every meaningful statistical category of play for his position at Texas. Ehlinger is currently the 2nd most prolific passer in Longhorn history (8,870 yards passing), trailing only Colt McCoy. His 68-22 touchdown-interception ratio is exemplary - in fact, the best ratio in Texas football history - with only 1.9% of his career attempts going for an interception. Ehlinger is also a dominant short yardage runner, tallying 1,526 rushing yards and 25 rushing touchdowns on quarterback draws, scrambles, and single wing power leads running over linebackers and safeties. He is the 3rd all-time leading rushing Longhorn quarterback, trailing only McCoy (by 45 yards) and the incomparable Vince Young, who, as one might guess, has a safe cushion in first place. Ehlinger has totaled a remarkable 93 total touchdowns running or passing in his Texas career - 2nd all-time - with a legitimate shot at surpassing Colt McCoy's epic 132 touchdown total. For fun and good measure, Sam has also caught 9 balls for 115 yards. His passing efficiency rating has gone up every year (124.1 as a true freshman, 146.8 as a sophomore, 151.8 as a junior) along with his accuracy (57.5%, 64.7%, 65.2%) and deep ball proficiency (7.0. 7.7, 8.1 yards per attempt).

In 2019, he threw for 3,663 yards and 32 touchdowns and 10 interceptions while compiling 663 yards rushing and 7 touchdowns on the ground. He was second only to Jalen Hurts in total yardage in Big 12 play. Sam has been a One-Man Gang in his time in Austin, as much from necessity as by design. More subjectively, he has proven himself to be intelligent, durable, strong as an ox, and a good leader. His accuracy, though spotty at times, has improved, and he is a quick learner in whom much can be invested should the coordinator be so inclined.

So, why then, do so many Longhorn fans bridle at the notion that he is an all-time Longhorn great quarterback? In fact, an all-timer at any position?

Wins.

Longhorn fans measure Texas quarterbacks in wins. The quarterback, win or lose, is the face of the program.

That is understandable on its face. Often the very best Texas quarterbacks played for the very best Texas teams. However, it is a correlative measure of quarterback efficacy and does not control for the total health of the program supporting that quarterback. One wonders how many wins Sam would put up playing behind the 2005 Texas offensive line, or throwing to the Big Three receivers, or running play action with Jamaal Charles or Ricky Williams in the backfield. Similarly, playing quarterback at the same time as Will Muschamp's 2009 defense or the Fred Akers units of the late 1970s and early 1980s is not a bad way to log some easy wins on the ledger, irrespective of how the offense plays that day. There were SEVENTEEN Texas Longhorns drafted in 1984. Sam has played with a total of nine NFL draft picks over his three years. Only three of them played on offense. A little perspective is healthy.

Last year, against the eventual national champion LSU Tigers, Ehlinger threw for 401 yards and four touchdowns, rushing for another 60 yards and a touchdown as well. No quarterback played better than Ehlinger against the Tigers (in fairness to Tua, Fields, and Lawrence, LSU's defense did get better as the season progressed) and his 461 total yards and five touchdowns powered the entire Longhorn effort. Play a little opportunistic defense and this would have gone down as an all-time quarterbacking performance. Should we hold it against Ehlinger that the Longhorn defense surrendered 45 points and 573 yards? Should he have played some safety?

Ehlinger's play in 2019 had rough moments, but you could also plainly see the deficiencies of Longhorn game planning and execution in his toughest outings: Oklahoma, TCU, and Baylor. The Longhorn offense looked unprepared and out of ideas. Giving up nine sacks to Oklahoma (Ehlinger had to carry the ball 23 times in that game), or coming out flat against TCU in the second half (Sam threw four picks in the contest), or simply laying up against Baylor, spoke to much larger issues outside of Ehlinger's control. Recall that a sophomore Vince Young was shut out against Oklahoma surrounded by a very talented offense with an offensive coordinator and head coach who had their own issues stepping up in that contest. Colt McCoy, after a brilliant redshirt freshman season, surrounded by the talented returning starters from a national champion, tossed 17 interceptions as a sophomore with a lesser supporting cast. That had many clamoring for a different field general. Yes, Start John Chiles really was a thing. Needless to say, Colt's 2008 changed a few minds. Quarterback is by far the most important position on the football field. Texas has a pretty damn good one. Top 5 all-time at Texas, in fact. But he needs more help. On the sidelines and between them.

Not so long-ago **Casey Thompson** was playing portal games (not to be confused with the video game Portal) to assuage the funk of being in a crowded quarterback room, but with the transfers of Shane Buechele and Cameron Rising, and the repurposing of Roschon Johnson to running back, he finds himself backing up Sam Ehlinger once again. Thompson saw spot action in 2019. He has repeatedly shown good running ability and mobility in the pocket, but how well he throws the ball remains the primary question. Is he good enough to win some games should the unthinkable happen? Thompson is older than his class designation (he was a 19-year-old high school senior) and that maturity will serve him well in fending off Hudson Card and Ja'Quinden Jackson.

True freshmen **Hudson Card** and **Ja'Quinden Jackson** will vie for their place in the quarterback depth chart. Both were highly recruited and each have contrasting strengths and styles. If either or both should exceed Casey Thompon's practice play, the coaches may still maintain a theoretical depth chart that keeps the more experienced Thompson listed on the second team. How it goes in game action could be a different story.

Prognosis

This is Sam Ehlinger's year. He is one of the most tenured, experienced quarterbacks in college football. Though he will throw to the most inexperienced group of receivers he has yet had at Texas, their talent level is not lacking, particularly if health pans out for a couple of key players. Similarly, it is reasonable to expect upgrades on the offensive line, at tight end, and at running back. The most important upgrade will be new offensive coordinator Mike Yurcich. The more passing game options and offensive ideas he can offer his senior quarterback, the more the Texas offense will profit.

Position Coach

Mike Yurcich is the quarterback coach and offensive coordinator for the Texas Longhorns. Yurcich rose to prominence at Oklahoma State in 2013 after serving as offensive coordinator at tiny Division II Shippensburg University, where his offense rewrote the school's record book. Mike Gundy famously found him on the internet, after seeking no-huddle, tempo-based offenses that could both run and throw the ball well. Yurcich was largely very productive at Oklahoma State, fielding multiple Top 20 offenses, including one of the best offenses in Cowboy school history in 2017 (ranked #2 nationally). Even more impressive was the following year when he turned career backup Taylor Cornelius into a highly productive quarterback despite all of the Cowboys star receivers departing to the NFL. Yurcich has a reputation for adaptability and innovation and he understands how to get the best out of personnel and formations. Texas upgraded.

Running Back

26	**Keaontay Ingram**	6-0	235	Junior

Rushing: 144-853 YARDS, 7 TDS, 5.9 YPC | Receiving: 29-242 YARDS, 3 TDS, 8.7 AVG

2	**Roschon Johnson**	6-1	215	Sophomore

Rushing: 123-665 YARDS, 7 TDS, 5.3 YPC | Receiving: 23-158 YARDS, 1 TDS, 6.9 AVG

32	**Daniel Young**	6-0	230	Senior

Rushing: 16-63 YARDS, 2 TDS, 3.9 YPC | Receiving: 2-7 YARDS

	Bijan Robinson	6-0	205	Freshman

Keaontay Ingram led the 2019 Longhorns in rushing, grabbed 29 passes, and tied Devin Duvernay with a team-leading ten touchdowns. He eclipsed 100+ yards rushing four times (Oklahoma State, Kansas, Kansas State, Utah) and finished the season in the Alamo Bowl against the aforementioned Utes with 134 yards from scrimmage, two touchdowns, and some highlight reel runs, reminding Longhorn faithful of what a rested, healthy Ingram is capable of doing. Unfortunately, that reminder was necessary. Ingram was rarely 100% throughout the 2019 season and, even when good to go, was most consistent in his inconsistency. Availability is a runner's most important ability and too frequently Ingram could not avail Texas with his ability for a full in-game work load. In Longhorn losses to LSU, Oklahoma and Iowa State he totaled only 47 rushing yards. In two years at Texas, Ingram has managed to amass 1,561 yards rushing at 5.5 yards per carry and added another 56 catches, but in those seasons his touch load capped out at 169 and 175, respectively. If he is going to break through the 250-touch barrier, it will require more durability than Longhorn coaches have seen to date.

Ingram is a medium speed slasher who excels on counters and cutbacks, is a capable blocker, and a fine receiver out of the backfield. His most important attributes are his balance, footwork and vision. Last year he demonstrated better power with a twenty-pound

offseason weight gain that took him to around 220 pounds. While seeking better durability with weight gain, it's important that Ingram also keep his weight where it best serves his native strengths as a runner. Offseason reports that he tips the scales at 235 pounds suggests that he could use a weight cut to enable sharper cuts on the field. Optimally, Keaontay would benefit from a split backfield and a 15-touch pitch count - something that a deep Longhorn running back room should be able to provide.

It's difficult to believe that true freshman **Roschon Johnson** could make the transition from star high school quarterback who dreamed of being the signal caller at the University of Texas to the team's #2 running back in a matter of weeks, but that speaks to his special character as well as Johnson's adaptability, overall athleticism, and unselfishness. As Johnson grew in his confidence and skill set, "Roschon runs pretty well for a quarterback" quickly evolved into "Roschon runs pretty well for a running back."

Johnson was a model of opportunity maximization throughout the season, compiling big games against West Virginia (21-121), Oklahoma (8-95), and Texas Tech (23-105-3 touchdowns). While Keaontay Ingram grabbed the primary reins in the bowl game against Utah, it's worth remembering that Johnson still averaged over 8 yards per carry in the contest. Throughout 2019, Roschon proved a talented runner, willing blocker, and demonstrated good hands as a receiving threat. Johnson shows a knack for finding and sensing space and revealed surprising quickness in his lateral cuts and acceleration. One area for improvement is in the ability to run through trash - not a Sooner reference - but rather the stray limbs and bumps that can cause a back to lose balance or decelerate when changing direction in or near the scrum. Given that RoJo had no experience at the position, his ability to accumulate 823 yards from scrimmage and score eight touchdowns on the season is no small feat. The fan favorite sophomore is just starting to blossom as a runner.

In 2017, a freshman **Daniel Young** displayed the most well-rounded skill set on the running back roster and his late season productivity (373 yards rushing at 4.6 yards per carry, 13 catches for 153 yards, 4 total touchdowns) and a strong bowl game against Missouri (112 total yards with a touchdown catch) suggested a bright future with more work on the horizon. It was not to be. As the running back talent improved around him, Young saw less work and even briefly struggled with ball security. Instead of exploring the transfer portal or consoling himself on social media with attention-seeking antics,

Young committed to doing the dirty work and being a great teammate and made the very best of what opportunities he got. Last season, a Texas Tech blowout allowed Young to feature his skills and he had eight carries for 41 yards and a touchdown in less than a quarter of action. Young is now a senior who has appeared in 35 games with five starts, totaling 589 rushing yards. A willing lead blocker and solid pass catcher, Young is capable of rising to the challenge if called upon to supplement a talented Longhorn backfield.

Bijan Robinson is a five-star recruit who will have his work cut out for him if he wants to claim his share of the touches in the running back room, but there is evidence that he is the kind of preternaturally gifted runner capable of doing just that.

Prognosis

It has long been a *Thinking Texas Football* maxim that running backs are more the product of their environment than their creator.

With that entered into the formal record, 2020 will feature the best running back talent, experience, and diversity of skill sets during the Tom Herman era. That may be damning with faint praise given recent history, but the talent trends in that position room and the supporting offensive landscape are all headed in the right direction, with the potential for a running back production leap in 2020. To understand where we are now, let's consider where we were.

2017 featured a four-headed backfield: Daniel Young, Chris Warren, Kyle Porter and Toneil Carter. Optimistic forecasters called this depth, but a canoe would scrape on those shallows. One of this book's Iron Laws warns: never confuse lots of familiar names with depth. Real depth is defined by talent, not the number of names on the chart. It bears mentioning that the unit also had a subpar offensive line and a generally miserable offensive ecosystem. No single runner amassed more than 400 yards rushing in a 13-game season and freshman Sam Ehlinger led the team in rushing.

Collectively, the unit totaled 288 carries for 1200 yards at 4.2 yards per carry and 16 touchdowns. Those season statistics, modest as they were, included 42 carries for 322 yards rushing at 7.7 yards per pop in a 56-0 win over San Jose State -- by far the worst team that Texas has played in the Herman era. Remove that game and Texas runners averaged a smooth 3.6 yards per carry and totaled 73 yards rushing per game as a unit. Chris Warren might have excelled as the #2 runner at Wisconsin, but he was ill-suited for 2017 Texas; Porter was a Katy program creation (with a laudable willingness to do some dirty work); Carter lacked physicality/focus, and Young was a true freshman with passable traits. For the season, Kyle Porter had the most attempts of the group, but averaged 3.1 yards per carry. One bright spot: the four-headed hydra totaled 43 receptions for 5 touchdowns

Tom Herman folded his 2017 running back cards and asked for a new deal. The cards dealt were steady graduate transfer Tre Watson and true freshman Keaontay Ingram. They immediately supplanted Kyle Porter and Daniel Young while Carter transferred out. Herman didn't draw pocket aces, but Texas could finally stay at the table. The duo totaled 370 carries for 1649 yards at 4.5 yards per carry, but the backfield's rushing touchdown total was more than doubled by Sam Ehlinger (16-7). Watson was the consistent work horse, amassing 786 yards on 185 carries (4.2) while young Ingram showed more explosiveness but less durability while amassing 708 yards at 5.0 yards per carry. Use in the passing game also increased, as Watson and Ingram both grabbed more than 20+ balls, grabbing 49 receptions between them. The Texas backfield had progressed from poor to passable.

In 2019, the unit took a meaningful leap forward, prompted by the physical maturation of sophomore Keaontay Ingram and the welcome addition of true freshman converted quarterback Roschon Johnson. Collectively, the entire unit went for 1568 yards on 283 carries and 17 touchdowns - good for a healthy 5.3 yards per carry average. Ingram totaled 853 yards rushing (5.9 per tote) while RoJo totaled 649 yards (5.3 a carry). Encouragingly, both Johnson and Ingram demonstrated quality in the passing game and the unit amassed 56 catches (Johnson and Ingram had 52 of them) - the first Herman era Longhorn backfield to break the 50-catch barrier. Texas finally had a good pair of running backs with developmental meat still left on the bone.

In 2020, Texas has two proven productive returning players in Johnson and Ingram, a stud incoming freshman X factor in Bijan Robinson, and senior veteran Daniel Young rounds out the mix. Senior, junior, sophomore, freshman. A pleasing symmetry of seniority. The Longhorns finally feature a backfield that most FBS teams would unhesitatingly trade for their own. The Horns also have an upgrade at offensive coordinator, an offensive line that should excel at run blocking, and a veteran team leader who can threaten the field with his arm and legs, and get the offense into favorable running game numbers. The blueprint for running game production is there. Can Texas execute against it? The most interesting unknown is Bijan Robinson, who boasts a skill set suggesting that a productive duo may need to make way for a troika. Managing a crowded backfield is a nice problem to have, but a Longhorn fan base that loves shiny new things means that any low touch Bijan Robinson games will be blamed for all offensive sputtering as well as global warming, fire ants, and a low yield sorghum crop. While running back production and efficiency markedly spiked in 2019, the unit's touch load actually declined from 2018. As Texas breaks in a new wide receiver corps and looks to put the ball into the hands of proven playmakers, expect the 2020 Texas runners to combine 2018 volume with 2019 levels of efficiency.

Position Coach

Stan Drayton began his 25-year coaching career at Allegheny (Pa.) College (1993) and he has mentored runners at Villanova (1996-00), Mississippi State (2004), Tennessee (2008) and Florida (2005-07, 2010) before serving as running backs coach at Ohio State (2011-14) where he crossed paths with Tom Herman. Drayton guided a pair of rookie runners to successful seasons with the Chicago Bears (2015-16) before rejoining the college ranks at Texas. With a reputation as a consummate teacher and a high-level recruiter, Drayton is a staff mainstay, but it took landing Bijan Robinson to address concerns about his ability to secure elite national runners.

Wide Receiver

13	**Brennan Eagles** 32-522 YARDS, 6 TDS, 16.3 AVG		6-3	230	Junior
21	**Jordan Whittington** 2-17 YARDS		6-1	215	Freshman (RS)
16	**Jake Smith** 25-274 YARDS, 6 TDS, 11 AVG		6-0	195	Sophomore
15	**Marcus Washington** 3-33 YARDS, 11 AVG		6-2	190	Sophomore
	Tarik Black		6-3	215	Senior
14	**Josh Moore**		6-1	175	Sophomore (RS)
84	**Kennedy Lewis**		6-3	200	Freshman (RS)
9	**Al'Vonte Woodard** 3-28 YARDS, 9.3 AVG		6-1	210	Sophomore (RS)
82	**Troy Omeire**		6-3	210	Freshman
	Dajon Harrison		5-10	170	Freshman
	Kelvontay Dixon		6-0	185	Freshman

Brennan Eagles is the most experienced returning receiver on the roster with only eight career starts and 23 game appearances. However, the third-year player, cast by necessity as an elder statesman in the wide receiver room, is still refining his craft and adding branches to a route tree that looked, at times, like a saguaro cactus. Eagles' soaring highs were comparable to the best of the record-setting band he shares his surname with - you know, everything featuring Joe Walsh - while his lows were reminiscent of the insipid *Witchy Woman* and their assorted elevator music. In five games Eagles was an intimidating game breaker, grabbing 19 balls for 408 yards and six touchdowns. In seven other appearances, he totaled 13 catches for 114 yards and was held out of the end zone. There was little rhyme or reason to that variation in output beyond the fact that Eagles struggled most with defenses that forced reads and route diversity. Feast or famine statistical variation is not uncommon for a #3 option deep threat receiver, but a couple of Eagles' quietest games came when the Texas offense was missing Collin Johnson and Devin Duvernay badly needed a bandmate to step up.

The physical attributes are indisputably there. The opportunity is golden. Eagles is bigger than most of the Longhorn linebacker room and one of the fastest Longhorns on the team. The junior appears to be the ready-made solution for the Longhorn offense at outside boundary receiver and is the sort of big bodied deep threat that offensive coordinator Mike Yurcich craves. Given that he also has reliable hands and there are few other clear challengers, 2020 ascension to the top of the box score as Sam Ehlinger's primary target seems fait accompli. However, immaturity has hampered his development at times. Eagles was suspended for conduct detrimental to the program before the TCU game and that one game suspension did not help the team's efforts or focus in the tumultuous week preceding that lackluster loss in Fort Worth. Eagles will need to avoid being grounded by bad habits if he wants to soar over Big 12 cornerbacks as the Longhorn's #1 receiver.

Jordan Whittington fits the football definition of potential energy. In the physical sciences, potential energy is stored energy or energy created by a position. For example, a boulder perched on the edge of a steep hill. At rest, an interesting land feature. But impotent. Remove the impediments at its base and offer a hearty push, and what was once static can transform into terrifying mayhem. Whittington is that boulder poised on that slope, waiting to unleash gridiron havoc. Unfortunately, complications from a sports hernia have been the impediment preventing that fulfillment of potential. If offseason reports are accurate and his latest corrective surgery can offer the right push, Texas will have a real asset to help power the Longhorn offense. Whittington is uniquely quick for his size and his ability to create space before and after the catch makes him a perfect fit for the slot position. Due to his size, he can also play through press coverage and operate as a ball carrier from the backfield. Whittington can improve on powering through first contact, which may be related to his prior health issues, but one of Whittington's assets is in his ability to avoid that contact to begin with. Whittington was slated to be a running back last year, a function of a desperate depth chart (Roschon Johnson was still taking quarterback snaps) but he spent most of his late high school career playing receiver, his forays into state championship game domination as a Wildcat quarterback notwithstanding. Whittington is a potential energizer that can line up anywhere and hunt for mismatches. The question is whether the Texas offense, a Philadelphia surgeon, and Texas S&C can get that boulder rolling.

Jake Smith flashed in his freshman season scoring six touchdowns (second only to Longhorn great Roy Williams in his true freshman debut) and demonstrated a nifty if erratic skill set. He tallied four touchdowns in his first four contests and the Arizona product showed the speed and quickness that made him the Gatorade Player of the Year coming out of high school, but he also struggled with consistency, dropping some key deep balls and experiencing enough misadventures as a punt returner that he was eventually shelved. Smith hit the freshman wall like a beltless crash test dummy in a Fiat. Smith was a do-everything player in high school against outmatched competition who spent more time at running back than receiver, so his understanding of the finer points of the position are still developing and that lack of experience likely compounded game day mental overload. Ineffective position coaching did not help matters either. The talented Smith needs a reset and the Texas offense aims to provide it. Jake is slated for the slot, but the new offensive staff is much more willing to move players around to find opportunity. In other words, if Jake Smith, Jordan Whittington and Josh Moore prove to be three of the best five receivers on the team, they will not log jam the slot and leave two assets kicking rocks and exploring the portal.

Tarik Black joins the team from Ann Arbor, Michigan and has two years of eligibility for the Longhorns. The Michigan graduate transfer is a former four-star high school recruit who could provide a valuable skill set and much needed leadership in a 6-3, 215-pound package. The 22-year-old made nine starts for the Wolverines and appeared in 20 games over the course of his career, but injuries to both feet have hampered what once looked like star quality promise. Black is very comfortable catching the ball in traffic and that will likely be his best use as injuries (broken feet in his freshman and sophomore seasons) degraded some of his explosiveness in his junior season. Whether his athleticism can be reclaimed is debatable but, encouragingly, Black was able to participate in twelve games in his junior year (5 starts, 25 catches, 323 yards), reversing a trend of early injury exits in years prior.

Texas badly needs maturity and reliability from a tough-minded athlete capable of shielding defenders and owning space on posts, ins, and curl routes from the Z position. Black is fully capable of fulfilling that role if healthy. Black totaled 40 catches for 507 yards over his career with his biggest game coming as a true freshman when he led the Wolverines in a season opening win over Florida. The Longhorns have had success with previous graduate transfers like Calvin Anderson, Parker Braun, and Tre Watson from both a production and leadership perspective and it is not unreasonable to speculate that a healthy Black is capable of catching 50+ balls in the Longhorn offense. Unfortunately, foot injuries have terminated or degraded many a promising athlete's career. Black should be an asset for Texas. The question is how valuable and for how long?

Marcus Washington lacks game experience, but the St Louis sophomore has one of the smoothest skill sets in the receiving corps and is arguably the most natural pass catcher on the roster. If he can reliably work the space created by Texas speed threats as the Z receiver, Washington has the potential to be a stick-moving 3rd down target who can also create chunk yardage in the early down play action RPO (Run-Pass Option) game. Washington will have to fend off multiple challengers for that role in the offense and the player who most quickly demonstrates knowledge of the playbook, decisive reads, and good hands will likely win the starting job.

Josh Moore missed all of last season with legal troubles and only played in six games in 2018 (and had 7 catches) before suffering a season ending injury, but the 3rd year sophomore has the raw talent to make a bid for a role in the wide receiver rotation. The long-armed, wiry receiver is quicker than fast, but he has shown excellent change of direction and acceleration. Moore is not a straight-line burner, but he has elite quickness, having tested at under a 4.0 second short shuttle with a 41.5-inch vertical leap. He is at his best in the slot, but is capable of playing in other spots. Durability, experience and prior off-field concerns are an issue, but Moore is an interesting potential dark horse contributor in an unproven wide receiver corp. His potential versatility allows him to back-up multiple positions and find work wherever it might present itself.

Kennedy Lewis returns to the program after a semester abroad at Austin Community College where he toured the exotic lands off of Riverside Drive. A rite of passage for many Texas students. Lewis is a big, fast athlete who has recorded a 10.53 100 meters as a high school prepster and he has the ideal 6-3 frame to offer a forgiving target radius to a deep ball chucking quarterback. Lewis is a great fit for the outside receiver X position, but the Melissa, Texas native's raw skill set requires tutelage and growth before he can supplant the incumbents.

Al'vonte Woodard broke his foot in early June of last year, but was able to come on late, securing rotation snaps over the last three games of the Longhorn season. Woodard is a big, physical receiver with the potential to play multiple positions, but the 3rd year sophomore has not yet had an opportunity to show his wares. Opportunity abounds for a big receiver who can run and Woodard could make an impact if he can progress at the nuts and bolts of the position.

Troy Omeire, **Kelvontay Dixon** and **Dajon Harrison** form a solid nucleus of freshmen. Omeire's physical maturity and strength could translate into early playing time depending on how things shake out in front of him. He is one to watch.

Prognosis

Sam Ehlinger has more career catches than all but two of his returning Longhorn receivers. The losses of Devin Duvernay and, to a lesser extent, an injured senior season from Collin Johnson, create a chasm of production and experience in the Longhorn receiving corps. The Texas offense loses more than sixty combined starts in addition to 2019 production totaling 144 catches, 1,945 yards, and 12 touchdowns. Fortunately, Moneyball theory and its associated football applications tells us that replacing a star does not require a 1:1 exchange. Incremental growth across a wide number of passing game targets can match the production loss of a stud. Do not look to one receiver to match Duvernay's production. Look to three. And more work for the tight ends and running backs in an offense that creates opportunity more broadly. By expanding the offense and growing each individual member, Texas can replace one of the most reliable breakout senior receivers in Longhorn history. That is the theory at least.

The unit does not lack for skill sets, speed, or raw athletic ability, but production and experience is slight and proven leadership is lacking. Fulfillment of potential, injuries, and simple maturity are also major factors in unit maximization. A focused Eagles, a healthy Whittington, a rejuvenated Tarik Black, Jake Smith coming on, and the emergence of a Marcus Washington or Josh Moore would mean a good receiving corps that could surpass all expectations. Ehlinger would enjoy a distributed target load and the offense would see improvement for the third consecutive year. Given improved position coaching, there is also some developmental hope, even absent much needed spring practices. However, a good bit of the upside in the receiving corps simply relies on too many unknowns. Fortunately, there is good historical evidence at Texas (and in the college and NFL game more broadly) that offenses with strong coordination, a very good quarterback, solid offensive line play, and quality running backs will generally give relatively unproven wide receivers the opportunity to rise to the occasion - en masse, or with notable individual breakouts.

In fact, there is a lengthy Longhorn tradition of this phenomenon.

In 1998, Wane McGarity starred for the Longhorns after his 1997 season ended early with a devastating knee injury. The 5th year senior gained 1087 receiving yards at 18.7 yards per catch, cementing McGarity as one of the premier deep threats in Texas history. Previously, a role player at best, he had never topped 315 yards in a season.

Jordan Shipley's theoretical talent level was always understood, but he spent six years in Austin, missing the entire 2004 and 2005 seasons due to injuries and contributing somewhat marginally in 2006 and 2007. Would Shipley ever regain his quickness and acceleration? That question - asked for four long years - was answered emphatically in his fifth and sixth seasons when the Ship finally came in. He exploded in 2008 and 2009, amassing 2,545 yards while grabbing 205 catches over two years. Shipley went from What Might Have Been to Longhorn Legend in quick order.

In 2007, little used senior Nate Jones (caught 13 only passes as a junior) became Colt McCoy's #1 receiver with 70 catches. Jones was not overwhelmingly talented, but was a maximizer afforded opportunity and attention.

Similarly, converted high school quarterback John Harris went from a third string receiver between 2011-2013 to a 1,000+ yard pass catcher in 2014 - the only bright spot in an otherwise moribund offense. His previous season high had been 141 yards. If you predicted John's emergence when he was running on the scout team in the spring of his senior year, send your Powerball predictions to me post-haste.

Finally, Devin Duvernay evolved from a steady junior - who some Longhorn faithful even considered a mild disappointment given his five-star recruiting pedigree -

into a 106 catch, 1386-yard senior superstar. Duvernay did not come out nowhere, but that season sure as hell did.

You may have noticed that all five unexpected breakout wide receivers were upperclassmen, often 4th and 5th year players, a couple of them recovering from major injuries with their careers largely written off. That suggests that seniority might be a key enabler. The young Longhorn receiving corps does not necessarily fit that profile. But Michigan transfer Tarik Black certainly does. On the roulette spin of production probability, put a bet on Black.

Position Coach(s)

Andre Coleman is the new wide receivers coach and this position should see a substantial upgrade. Coleman was an analyst at Texas before his promotion, but he has been both a former passing game coordinator and receivers coach at Kansas State. Andre won over the team and Herman with his coaching before the Alamo Bowl and he is known as a detail-oriented position coach who should immediately upgrade the level of coaching that preceded him. Coleman was also a brilliant college and NFL returner. He can certainly help that part of the Texas special teams. His biggest adjustment will be found in recruiting, where he will need to acclimatize to the national stage.

Tight End

80	Cade Brewer	6-3	250	Senior
	11-159 YARDS, 1 TD, 14.5 AVG			
18	Jared Wiley	6-6	255	Sophomore
	1-15 YARDS			
85	Malcolm Epps	6-6	250	Sophomore
	20-232 YARDS, 2 TDS, 11.6 AVG			
89	Brayden Liebrock	6-4	235	Freshman (RS)

Cade Brewer earned playing time as a true freshman in 2017 before a late ACL injury robbed him of the remainder of his season. In 2018, the preview was not sanguine about his ability to rebound to form and unfortunately that proved correct. He played in all 14 games, but was largely a non-factor backing up Andrew Beck. Brewer put on weight, not all of it necessarily good, and he was a step slower and unable to get in and out of his breaks the way he did as a freshman. Fortunately, Brewer recovered form in 2019, but lost four starts with an ankle injury against TCU, gutting it out after surgery to return against Utah. While his receiving contributions were relatively marginal, the junior Brewer was moving better, carrying his weight better, and showed some improvement as a blocker. Now a senior flanked by an unproven receiving corps, it is a good bet that Brewer will be asked to provide consistency, good routes and some chain-moving for the Longhorn offense. The veteran Brewer has appeared in 33 games with 12 starts while compiling 22 career catches. He could very well match or exceed that career output in his senior season.

Jared Wiley did not get the benefit of a needed redshirt season, but two starts and participation in twelve games did grant some experience. A starved depth chart meant that Texas simply needed another body at tight end, so there is no blame to assess. Though well along in his physical development, the imposing former high school quarterback is still learning blocking technique, attacking the weight room, and increasing his comfort as a pass catcher. Wiley still has a very favorable long-term path for development with his best upside as a 6-6, 270-pound physical monster at the point of attack with enough speed and pass catching ability to punish a defense in the red zone or on play action. Wiley should be the guy when Texas decides they want to hammer the running game, but he can expand that blocking role by demonstrating that he can operate both as a move tight end (used as a lead blocker from the backfield, not always easy for taller guys) as well as a traditional in-line blocker taking on defensive ends and outside linebackers.

Malcolm Epps moves from wide receiver to tight end after catching 20 balls on the outside last year. It's a better fit for the 6-6, 245-pound former basketball player, who often struggled to separate. Epps has an 82-inch wingspan and while he will struggle to block linebackers and defensive ends at the point of attack, he should see a good bit of his playing time in a flexed role. Particularly if the wide receiver corps demonstrates a lack of big body reliability. Malcolm can be effective when he draws the right coverage match-ups. Epps has a long way to go with respect to building out the strength and power to be a true multifaceted every down tight end role, but the third-year sophomore has plenty of time remaining to explore his ceiling.

Brayden Liebrock getting a redshirt last season was a program win. He put on good weight and the highly recruited Arizona native will continue to build out his frame to complement a fluid receiving skill set. August camp will tell us quickly if Liebrock has the physicality and size to hold up in all phases of the position and it is not unreasonable to think that he could begin chipping in soon as a passing game asset. Liebrock has rare pass-catching skills and soft hands. Now it's about getting him some game action.

Prognosis

Last year's tight end depth chart was an argument for more four wide receiver sets, but recruiting and development continue to steadily progress the talent level at the position. Ideally, the Longhorn offense wants a complete tight end who can block from the backfield as a de facto fullback when needed, put a hand in the dirt and win the edge against a defensive end, flex out and create a credible pass catching threat, and has the athleticism to create a viable play action threat on standard downs. Since Rob Gronkowski is unavailable, Texas would gladly settle for a specialist or two who thrive either as a pass catcher or run blocker. Programs as geographically and culturally disparate as Miami, Iowa, Notre Dame, Stanford, and Oklahoma have demonstrated a knack for maximizing the tight end position due to their offensive utilization, recruiting, and talent development. The Catch 22 of the position is that it is difficult to sell a recruit without a history of tight end production and tight end production is difficult to manufacture without great tight end recruits. You break the cycle with development, informing the best recruits, "Look what we are getting done with this athletically limited guy, imagine what you could do for us, Captain Hotshot." That was just an example. Texas will not start a player named Captain Hotshot. But a Major Applewhite...

Texas is probably a year out from seeing a jump in tight end play, but expect a bump in 2020.

Position Coach

Former Longhorn offensive lineman Jay Boulware returns to Texas after a long winding road through programs as diverse as Arizona, Stanford, Utah, Iowa State, Auburn, and Oklahoma. He has coached both running backs and tight ends and has held multiple special teams coordinator positions. Boulware is a smart hire who should be an asset across the board.

Offensive Line

52	Samuel Cosmi	OT	6-6	310	Junior (RS)
68	Derek Kerstetter	C	6-5	305	Senior
75	Junior Angilau	OG	6-6	300	Sophomore (RS)
70	Christian Jones	OT	6-6	305	Sophomore (RS)
78	Denzel Okafor	OG	6-4	315	Senior (RS)
72	Tyler Johnson	OG	6-6	325	Freshman (RS)
73	Isaiah Hookfin	OT	6-5	295	Freshman (RS)
67	Tope Imade	OG	6-6	350	Senior (RS)
55	Willie Tyler	OT	6-7	330	Sophomore (RS)
76	Reese Moore	OT	6-7	285	Sophomore (RS)
74	Rafiti Ghirmai	C	6-5	320	Sophomore (RS)

71	Logan Parr	OG	6-4	295	Freshman
65	Jake Majors	OL	6-3	310	Freshman
	Jaylen Garth	OL	6-5	290	Freshman
	Andrej Karic	OL	6-6	280	Freshman

Sam Cosmi enters his fourth year at Texas after redshirting as a freshman. The preseason All-American has already started 26 games for the Longhorns and should shine in his likely final junior season. Cosmi was an undersized starter as a redshirt freshman, but a great motor, a good strength base, and unfiltered aggression made him one of the Big 12's best tackles and the standout performer of the 2018 Longhorn offensive line. 2019 revealed a heavier, more powerful athlete who could better anchor against pass rushers, but Cosmi still maintained the sweet feet that will make him a first round NFL draft pick. Sam is a dynamic athlete, recording testing numbers for Yancy McKnight that match the sorts of metrics one typically sees from standout defensive linemen. Gifted with elite "get-off" at his position, a 310-pound Cosmi recorded a 1.72 second 10-yard sprint during winter conditioning - a number that compares favorably with Pro Bowl NFL defensive end Joey Bosa, who recorded a 1.69 second 10-yard split at the NFL combine. Given that Cosmi has Bosa by forty pounds and Bosa had just spent the last eight weeks specifically training for his run, the true dimensions of Cosmi's athleticism and ability to accelerate start to take form.

Cosmi's athleticism was also more humorously and joyously evidenced by his trick play touchdown against West Virginia. The big man took an outside lateral inside the West Virginia red zone, made a sharp cut behind his blocker, and then accelerated for the pylon, barreling through a West Virginia tackler like a prime Earl Campbell. Everyone loves a Big Man Touchdown and

Cosmi rightfully dominated the highlights that Saturday. Cosmi will serve as the catalyst for, rather than the scorer of, multiple 2020 touchdowns and to that end Sam has always been a good blocker in space and excels at finding and erasing smaller defenders, but he is now also capable of moving the line of scrimmage at the sharp end of the point of attack, displacing big bodies rather than just screening or turning a defender's shoulder. Left tackle is in good hands and the two Sams are the most important foundational pieces of the Texas Longhorn offense.

Derek Kerstetter has started 28 games in his Longhorn career with the Swiss Army knife veteran seeing starting time at right tackle (24 starts) and guard (4 starts). To complete the full offensive line trifecta, Kerstetter will likely answer the call in his final Longhorn season at center. That move is not motivated by any failings at his previous position - according to Pro Football Focus, Kerstetter and Cosmi were the only returning tackle duo with a mean pass blocking grade of 85 or better amongst all Power Five conference schools. Kerstetter even graded out at an excellent 91.6 as a pass blocker, albeit without facing the best edge rusher on the opposing defense. However, despite his pass blocking acumen, Kerstetter is the best utility asset on the roster, with the ability to capably play all of the offensive line positions, so expect Herb Hand to use him where needed to create the best starting five possible. Right now, the staff believes that is Kerstetter snapping the ball to Sam Ehlinger, assuming some of his offensive line brethren can lock down right tackle. Kerstetter has a tackle's body

which means a high natural base and he can struggle getting displacement on squatty defenders on initial contact, but he is very good on the pull, demonstrates live feet, does a good job of preventing pass rushers from getting to their second move, and is skilled at walling off backside defenders. He also possesses a high football IQ with a strong attention to detail. Line calls will pose little concern for him, but high-end nose tackles may be a handful if he cannot keep his pads and hips down. Keondre Coburn and T'Vondre Sweat will certainly keep him busy in practice. We learned early in Kerstetter's career that competitiveness and a team-first mentality define his athletic character. Recall that Derek was forced into action in 2017 as a true freshman and started ten games at right tackle for a truly bad offense. He learned to swim in piranha infested waters wearing water wings made of razor blades, but he never stopped fighting, even when outmatched. Now a seasoned, reliable veteran, Kerstetter brings leadership and stability to an offensive line that must demonstrate better consistency and cohesion.

Redshirt freshman **Junior Angilau** replaced long time starter Patrick Vahe at guard last season and there was little to no drop off in overall performance. Now seasoned by twelve starts, the third-year guard is ready to bring his physicality to bear on Longhorn opponents. Junior missed the second half of the Kansas State game and all of the Iowa State contest with a MCL strain, but gutted it out to return quickly and finish the year in quite a bit of pain. Angilau's willingness to rehab aggressively and play through considerable discomfort earned him respect from staff and teammates alike. Angilau is deceptively long and lean for a guard and despite his height, he can demonstrate excellent punch at the point of attack when he keeps his pads down. Consistency and avoiding lunging at defenders will be key to his third-year progress. With square shoulders, a good base, and better reach than all of the defenders he will face, Junior is not going to lose many fights in a phone booth. He must stop beating himself with overreach. Quicker stunting defenders sometimes gave him fits (see Oklahoma, Baylor, West Virginia games) by exploiting that tendency, particularly in pass protection. Against physical power-oriented defensive lines, Angilau was frequently outstanding. He played particularly well in the bowl game against a Utah defensive line packed with NFL draft picks. Angilau can run and is a very capable blocker on the move. He has tremendous growth potential if he can shore up his pass protection with more consistent technique. He will be a net asset as a run blocker.

Christian Jones did not play football until his junior year of high school, preferring soccer. But when you are 6-5 and carved out of granite, the Lionel Messi posters generally get replaced by Tyron Smith. By his senior year, Jones was a team captain and a high-level two-way player (many of his best offers were on defense) who operated a bit under-the-radar from the national recruiting services, but was coveted by the programs who pride themselves on discovering diamonds in the rough. Fortunately, Texas did their Greater Houston due diligence and landed their man. At Cypress Woods, Jones

played in a run first offense and developed few skills as a pass blocker. He also saw little game action outside of special teams as a redshirt freshman at Texas. So the seemingly puzzling preseason push to move right tackle Derek Kerstetter to center suggests that the offensive staff knows some things that we do not about Jones or one of his young peers. Either that, or a mischievous raccoon broke into Herman's Excel depth chart spreadsheet and tinkered with the cells. The coaches knowing things we don't scenario seems more probable, though that raccoon likely devised last year's game plan against OU. To date, no one can explain why the line practiced knocking over garbage bins rather than watching film on Alex Grinch's favorite line stunts. If Jones can continue his steep learning curve and marry those soccer feet to his First Guy Off Of The Bus frame, Texas may have a very pleasant surprise at right tackle. Either way - whether starter or key backup - Jones is about to take a massive jump in responsibility.

Fifth year senior **Denzel Okafor** has had a good long soak in the developmental tub and it is time for the veteran to show the results in his final season after 39 game appearances and five starts over his Longhorn career. Okafor wasted a needed developmental redshirt in his freshman year with a handful of meaningless snaps as Texas football choked on the dying fumes of the Strong era. His developmental timeline never really caught up. In 2017, he was thrust unprepared into the spotlight at offensive tackle as his tackle peers began to mirror the fate of the drummers in *Spinal Tap*. Undeveloped, likely out of position, and without a learning base to draw from, Okafor struggled badly in four starts. Okafor is not a natural pass protector at right tackle, but he can be a plus performer in the running game and is capable of meeting the more forgiving pass blocking requirements found at guard. Okafor is a very powerful if somewhat stiff athlete, but he will be a valuable starter or first man off of the bench in 2020.

Tyler Johnson is someone to keep an eye on. The Alief Elsik product is physically gifted and dispositionally sound (low drama, good grades, serious about football - the offensive lineman Holy Trinity). His success seems a matter of when and where rather than if. The staff wisely redshirted the blue-chip recruit and he will compete for a starting role with Denzel Okafor at right guard. Johnson is ahead of the game as a no-nonsense drive blocker, but he will need to add some technical skills and experience to hold up in the position's other requirements. Though he played tackle in high school, the data is not yet apparent whether he is capable of holding down right tackle at some future date. Meanwhile, Johnson is versatile enough to play inside, gain experience, and serve as a key man off of the bench, if not earn the outright starting nod at right guard during August camp.

Isaiah Hookfin redshirted last season, allowing the once underweight high school senior to add strength and size to a very athletic frame. Mission accomplished and still ongoing. Along the way he earned praise from fellow players and coaches for his quiet, serious approach to training and development. Hookfin was considered a somewhat marginal recruit until late in his senior season when the late bloomer's film started to make the rounds and college evaluators remembered that adding weight and strength to a big-framed and gifted athlete is not very difficult, particularly given that 18 year olds tend to get larger when they eat and lift a lot. Late suitors began to parachute in like the 82nd Airborne at Market Garden, but Hookfin threw in with the division in Austin. Hookfin is blessed with natural fluidity, flexible hips, and coordination that belies a body a cinnamon roll short of 300 bills. Now he just needs to add more strength, technical proficiency, and continue to feed his mean streak. Hookfin could legitimately compete for a starting role at right tackle and, failing that, should secure a role and the commensurate developmental snaps that come with being one of the top eight offensive linemen on the depth chart.

Tope Imade is tied for the heaviest player on the team with fellow 350 pounder Keondre Coburn. This raises the weighty question (and in raising it: use your knees, not your back) of whether Imade weighs 1.0 Coburns or Coburn weighs a full Imade. The question is moot as the answer won't help any ferris wheel operators, or the exhausted line cooks at the Chinese buffet, will it? Imade is a powerful athlete who carries 350 pounds well on his 6-6 frame, but the fourth-year offensive lineman has not yet made a dent in playing time on special teams, much less the offensive line rotation. The Longhorn staff would love to see Imade assert himself with a full Coburn of effort.

Big **Willie Tyler** redshirted after transferring from Iowa Western Community College where he starred as a freshman for a 10-1 team. The Wisconsin native still has three years of eligibility at Texas, having accumulated sufficient credits and academic standing to allow him to transfer after that first season. That unanticipated development allowed Tyler to fly under the JUCO recruiting radar as it was assumed he would complete his sophomore season before matriculating to a four year institution. Tyler needed time to reshape his body and the redshirt season with Yancy McKnight served him well in that regard. Though his size suggests offensive tackle, Tyler will get a serious look at guard before the coaches make a final determination on his best fit.

Reese Moore continues his 3rd year walking the developmental path like Cain in *Kung Fu*. The former tight end and multi-sport athlete from Seminole has athletic attributes, but entering his third year after a redshirt and an uneventful redshirt freshman campaign last year, world events deprived him of the opportunity to showcase any improvement in the spring. He will get his chance in August.

Third year sophomore **Rafiti Ghirmai** saw limited snaps last year with three brief game appearances in blowout wins, but he is currently slated as the second team center. The former high school left tackle had a slow adjustment to center and wasn't afforded the opportunity to redeem a rough 2018 Spring debut where he socially distanced several snaps away from Longhorn quarterbacks. Ghirmai will compete with the incoming freshmen for his back-up role.

Jake Majors, **Logan Parr**, **Andrej Karic** and **Jaylen Garth** form the nucleus of a solid incoming recruiting class. Expect all four freshmen to redshirt absent bad luck.

Prognosis

The Texas offensive line currently boasts 15 names: Kerstetter, Cosmi, Angilau, Jones, Okafor, Johnson, Hookfin, Imade, Moore, Ghirmai, Tyler, Parr, Majors, Garth, and Karic.

Which of them is not like the other? Hint: you can or will be able to add the letters RS after every single one of those names save one athlete. That would be jack-of-all-trades Derek Kerstetter. The 2017 freshman offensive tackle that Texas threw into the deep end of the swimming pool wearing full pads to see if he could swim. When 14 of 15 offensive linemen in a program can redshirt, the program is putting money in the bank instead of leasing a car with the proceeds from a home equity loan. Building on a solid foundation instead of a Jenga tower of debt, where the removal of a key piece or two has it all come crashing down. Texas fans have seen the effects of an offensive line crash multiple times in recent memory and it is not a pretty sight. Even when immediate needs are dire and a staff deludes itself that a true freshman offensive lineman might swing a game result, once you start overspending on your credit card instead of putting money in savings, you can never get back on the positive side of the ledger. At some point, you have to take your lumps and do what's right for the zlong-term viability of the program.

As for 2020, Texas wants its most reliable veterans at left tackle (the most important pass blocker) and center (coordinates the line calls). After slotting Cosmi and Kerstetter accordingly, it is easy to write in returning starting guard Junior Angilau on the left next to Cosmi. With those bases covered, Herb Hand will have the task of building out the right side of his offensive line with the best combinations resulting from battles between Okafor vs. Johnson vs. Tyler at right guard and Jones vs. Hookfin at right tackle. If Okafor enters into the right tackle mix, you will know that neither Jones nor Hookfin inspired sufficient staff confidence and Tyler Johnson probably drew just enough. Irrespective of the mix, this should be a pretty capable run blocking offensive line. That is a nice luxury to have, but the upside of the unit and the entire Texas offense will be realized by the offensive line's ability to pass protect against higher order defenses. They failed too often in that task last year, surrendering the second most sacks in the Big 12 and far too many pressures, particularly over the second half of the season.

Position Coach

Herb Hand sounds like a product sold in the garden section of Home Depot, but after Texas surrendered 36 sacks in 13 games and nine sacks against bitter rival OU last year, Texas fans are looking for some Miracle Gro. The Longhorn offensive line was not helped by weak game planning and Ehlinger held on to a few balls too many, but the popular Hand cannot escape criticism for a unit that was dominated in conference match-ups against Oklahoma and Baylor. An avid foodie and old school rap enthusiast, the charismatic Hand is regarded as one of the early innovators of the smash mouth spread in his stints at West Virginia, Tulsa and Auburn, but he has a reputation - fair or not - for his units struggling against stunts and line games. Hand was retained after the offseason staff cleaning. He needs to repay his head coach's confidence with a strong 2020.

Defensive Overview

DFEI Defense Ratings (DFEI) represent the per possession scoring advantage a team's defense would be expected to have on a neutral field against an average offense. Schedule strength is represented by each team's average per possession defensive opponent adjustment. It calculates the percentage of opponent offensive drives that result in a touchdown or at least one first down, total yards surrendered by the defense divided by the total yards available to be earned based on starting field position, the percentage of opponent offensive drives that average at least ten yards per play, the percentage of opponent offensive drives that earn zero or negative yards, and the percentage of opponent offensive drives that result in a fumble or interception.

Year	Defensive Rank	Coordinator	Record
2008	4	Will Muschamp	12-1
2009	3	Will Muschamp	13-1
2010	26	Will Muschamp	5-7
2011	6	Manny Diaz	8-5
2012	63	Manny Diaz	9-4
2013	23	Manny Diaz / Greg Robinson	8-5
2014	13	Vance Bedford	6-7
2015	47	Vance Bedford	5-7
2016	51	Vance Bedford	5-7
2017	7	Todd Orlando	7-6
2018	44	Todd Orlando	10-4
2019	54	Todd Orlando	8-5

Over the last twelve years, Texas has had five defensive coordinators. In 2020, Chris Ash will make six. Texas coordinator epochs have gone largely in blocks of three years, with Greg Robinson serving less than a full season as a temporary stopgap. Even given that inconsistency, Texas has still managed four top 10 defenses in that span. As well as three additional top 26 finishes. Yet, Texas has lost at least four games per season for ten years running. That suggests that while defense is important, winning in modern football defies the old adage that defense wins championships. Sometimes it does. But several times at Texas, fielding an elite defense did not even result in a winning season. What can we learn about the past that will inform the future? There are some patterns worth examining.

In the last decade plus, Texas has had only one A level defensive coordinator: Will Muschamp. It is no coincidence that he was also the best teacher of the game, had the soundest philosophical approach against spread offenses, and commanded the most respect from his staff and players. He was also a good linebacker coach, which cannot be underestimated in evaluating the totality of a defensive coordinator's performance. The coordinator's own position group coaching is always key and far too many defensive coordinators fall into the trap of the college professor who falls in love with research or publication at the expense of their classroom teaching. Despite the colorful sound bytes and sideline intensity, Muschamp was first and foremost a teacher and related concepts in ways that the players understood. He also did an excellent job of managing the defensive staff, forcing them to emphasize the teaching aspects of the game that he valued most. The fact that he could credibly coach any position on the defense only reinforced his standing. A coordinator's ability to know what good looks like from every position group is a powerful guarantor of quality control. Crucially, Muschamp understood that his schemes and machinations were irrelevant without giving his players the proper positional tools. Muschamp's skill set - and impatience with nonsense - were also his primary source of tension with Mack Brown and a program on cruise control. The official story is that Muschamp left Austin for a Top 10 head coaching job at Florida. The reality is that he left Texas and a head-coach-in-waiting promise because he knew Brown was going nowhere soon and the head coach was increasingly becoming a figurehead uninterested in the grind of program building. In three short years, Muschamp fielded two elite defenses, a pretty good one, and then set the table nicely for his successor.

In 2011, Manny Diaz inherited a loaded Muschamp defense and did a fine job with the pieces assembled by his predecessor. Experienced linebackers (Keenan Robinson, Manny Acho) were key to the execution of his disruption-based defense and he held down opponent passing attacks with excellent upperclassmen defensive backs running schemes the Big 12 had not yet really seen. The Mack Brown program management issues that drove Muschamp away also weighed on Diaz, who fought for more contact in practice, more aggressive camps, and more staff discipline from his senior assistants; some simply refused to get on board or properly teach the Cover 3 match-up zone base principles that Diaz espoused. The lack of physicality and tackling in practice showed up in his second season. The defense unraveled painfully in 2012 and Diaz was fired in the early part of the 2013 season after his defense gave up a staggering 550 yards of rushing to the BYU Cougars. Did Taysom Hill just score again? Diaz's greatest mistake was trying to compensate for a lack of positional teaching and practice intensity with defensive calls that turned the players into robotic X's trying to outguess the offensive O's. Get used to identifying that pattern as we go along. Unlike Todd Orlando, Diaz largely limited that tendency to the front seven, but Texas run fits still looked like a triple divorcee trying to fit into her high school hot pants after her third day at Jenny Craig. To Diaz's credit, he was one of the most open, approachable, and self-critical coordinators in Texas history. He knew the program was complacent and self-satisfied, but he tried a tactical approach to solve a strategic problem. It is revealing that Diaz has had defensive success at pretty much every program stop he has ever made: Middle Tennessee State, Mississippi State, Louisiana Tech, Mississippi State again, and Miami. All except for the final days of the Brown era. Just as failing coordinators can sabotage good head coaches, stubborn head coaches can certainly return the favor.

Veteran Greg Robinson, former Longhorn co-defensive coordinator in 2004, was brought in as a defensive analyst before the 2013 season (cough cough Diaz firing insurance cough cough) and did a solid job salvaging that defense in his single season as defensive coordinator. He took the KISS principle and gave the entire defense a big 'ol smooch. He was also granted the in-season tackling and practice tempo from Brown that Diaz had begged for and he used that time to focus almost entirely on fundamentals, positional teaching, and very simple schemes. There were a lot of 6A Texas high schools running more complex stuff than the Longhorns (Texas was still running a base 4-3 on 3rd and 6 against most opponents) in 2013, but Robinson's focus on the basics paid off with better defense. Dated and predictable will not fly against the highest-level modern offenses, but Robinson served as a fine stop gap. More importantly, his time was clear proof that teaching the game broadly always trumps teaching calls.

Vance Bedford (and Charlie Strong) coordinated the 2014 Longhorns. They inherited a talented, veteran defensive group and did a good job playing a strong hand. Sound familiar? One season highlight was their terrific game plan for national passing leader Baylor built on multiple, shifting pre-snap looks. Bears quarterback Bryce Petty went 7 of 22 for 111 yards, but a hopeless Texas offense frittered away the effort. Still, it was a promising defensive season, powered by a senior-laden defense. That defensive success was short lived. When those six key seniors departed (Diggs, Thompson, Hicks, Edmond, Reed, Brown) the Longhorns struggled to fill the gap and the 2015 and 2016 Longhorns were too schematically simple, poorly organized, and foolish on the field. They were known for mindless penalties on key downs, blown assignments, and pointless gambles.

Bedford began to resort to default blitzing or simplistic drop coverages in lieu of teaching the game or raising positional IQ. In the last two years of the Strong run, the defense could still overwhelm bad offenses with good Longhorn athletes, but their obliteration by better opponents was as predictable as it was thorough. The takeaways from the Strong/Bedford era? When a defensive coordinator inherits a lot of good veteran talent on defense, do not assume that the honeymoon year is predictive. We also see another group of coaches transition poorly from a player-led veteran defense to a self-defeating, blitz-heavy, X's running to spots, let's-throw-something-at-the-wall approach when they prove incapable or unwilling to educate their young defenders. A fundamental failure to teach the game caught up to yet another Texas coaching staff.

Finally, Todd Orlando. Well-liked. A stand-up guy. Great command of the room. His players respected him. He had success at Utah State and Houston. He came in with extraordinary promise and, after a gangbusters first season, there were proclamations of a coming decade of defensive dominance. Stop me if you know this part: he had a dominant debut with excellent inherited veteran talent running a new look defense (a borrowed fusion from Iowa State defensive coordinator Jon Heacock) that conference offenses had not yet adjusted to, followed immediately by a significant step back in his second year as Big 12 offenses caught up, key experienced veterans (Ford, Jefferson, Elliott, Hill, Hall) left, and, in the absence of development, or even establishing a base defensive identity, Orlando and his staff began to increasingly rely on call matching.

Call matching is the kinder description for what it really is: Gridiron Battleship. Like the board game, it is a series of blind guesses, hoping to hit on something out there in the vast ocean to target your next bombardment. I-9, dual safety blitz? No. B-6, delayed free safety blitz? No. A-4, nickel and cornerback blitz, while Ossai covers the slot receiver? No. Meanwhile, the Texas fleet is on the bottom of the ocean. Teaching calls instead of the precepts of the game never works and running "looks" is not a defensive philosophy. Decentralized command is not just a tool for enriching economies, running a successful company, or ensuring the success of a military mission. It is the only way pupils can grow and develop their own skills to apply on game day. Modern offenses no longer ask defenses true-false questions on a Scantron. They ask for essays. Written on the spot. Demanding subject matter mastery. Not rote memorization. If players are not empowered to think and do not possess the tools to play their position while honoring the fundamentals of the game, they will be exposed.

Gridiron Battleship turns defenders into puppets on a string instead of thinking actors who can react to what they see unfolding before them within the larger scheme. Aesthetically pleasing, entirely theoretical, orchestrated defensive personnel movements are rendered useless if the offense has the audacity to actually do what they want instead of what the defensive coordinator expects. By Orlando's third year, Tom Herman brought in Chris Ash in October as a helpful consultant (cough cough firing insurance cough cough) and with Orlando's behaviors undeterred, his fate was decided. When a head coach brings in a former defensive coordinator colleague who shared a national title run with him to offer some thoughts while his current defensive coordinator is failing, well, read the Helvetica Bold on the wall. It is a bit like a husband flying in his ex-girlfriend to give his wife some input on their failing marriage. "Honey, you remember Sherri. She's going to live with us for a while. Follow you around. Just offer helpful tips and stuff. Don't feel threatened."

So, ends yet another three-year run for a Longhorn defensive coordinator. The headstones of the Texas defensive coordinator graveyard all share the same epitaph: "Here Rests (fill in the blank) For He Failed to Teach and Develop." It is worth Tom Herman and Chris Ash's time to stroll through that solemn yard, put down a few wreaths, and reflect.

What can we reflect on concerning the unit's 2019 failures that might help us better understand 2020 upside?

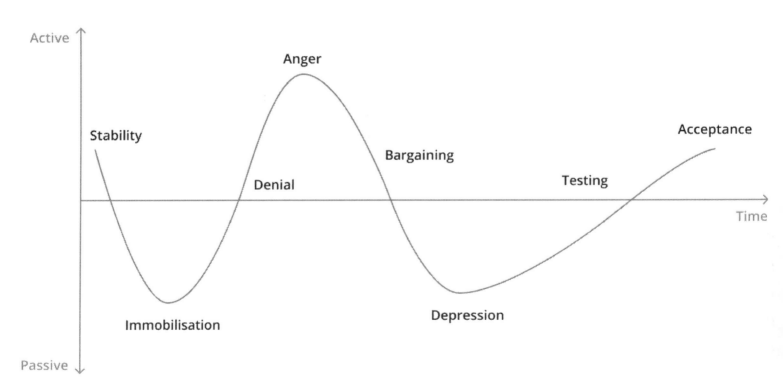

What is the Kubler-Ross model for the Stages of Grief doing in the defensive section of a football preview? Oh, you already know. Denial is the third phase. You should be in Acceptance by now. If you bought the 2019 prospectus, we already know that you are smart, likable, and discerning. You were also well-served by its call out of Orlando's 2018 bad habits. Something was rotten in Denmark in how he was calling defenses trying to compensate for inexperienced or untaught players. Despite what the coaches tried to tell us, it was not "just injuries." Trying to put athletes on a joystick tethered to the sideline is never a good habit.

From the 2019 Prospectus on Orlando's call matching:

*"**Call Matching.** While defensive coordinators are constantly challenged by personnel and formation variations and have to make educated inferences based on offensive field position, down and distance, tendency and formation, they can get into the very bad habit of anticipatory call matching. More than just guessing a likely offensive approach, they try to orchestrate the perfect defense, blitz or wrinkle for a gotcha play call rather than relying on the defense's underlying discipline and structure that allows player instinct and knowledge to make real time adjustments. The solution to the pressure that offenses can put on a defense is not outguessing them. It is not a game of Battleship. It is teaching players football principles within the construct of the defense and letting them do their jobs."*

You were less well-served by this preview's prediction that the Texas staff would rationally assess, self-reflect, self-correct, establish a core identity base defense, renew focus on fundamentals, and put players in the right roles. None of that occurred. Bad habits got worse and spring and fall practices were effectively wasted. The rational actor model of analysis can be naive when it assumes that others, in this case, professional football coaches, perceive glaring issues the same way you do. I have had better luck guessing how a kitten will react to a ball of yarn covered in laser pointers on a floor draped in

double-sided scotch tape than trying to get in the heads of that 2019 Longhorn staff.

Thus the 2019 Texas defense - overrun with top level athletes - was one of the three worst defenses in the Big 12. Just beating out Kansas and Texas Tech. Just beating out Kansas and Texas Tech in defense is like edging Chris Christie teamed with a tree sloth in a three-legged race with Usain Bolt as your partner. Put that participation medal at the bottom of your sock drawer and never speak of it again.

The Texas defense surrendered 27.5 points per game and opponents tallied 6.1 yards per play. The Texas pass defense allowed at least one completion of 45+ yards in every game except the opener against Louisiana Tech and the bowl game against Utah. The Utah game plan was devised in eight practices by an interim staff and Louisiana Tech plays its conference schedule against the likes of UTEP, North Texas, and Rice. As Tom Herman likes to say,"Winning is hard." Indeed. Winning for the defense got easier the fewer interactions they had with staff. Beating you over the head with every statistical inadequacy will serve nothing but to get this preview flung against your living room (let's be realistic, bathroom) wall, but examining Big 12 play allows an apples-to-apples comparison with a full conference round robin. In that format, a Burnt Orange worm-filled defensive apple gave up 6.2 yards per snap and 456 yards per game. Texas got no pressure on the opposing quarterback (2nd to last in the conference in sacks, bottom third in pressure rate) despite constant blitzing, had a middling rush defense despite a good run-stopping defensive line with quality depth, and opposing passers compiled a strong 141 passing efficiency ranking. Personnel were misused, poorly taught, and there was no discernible base defense until around Game 9 of the season. Fundamentals across the board were atrocious. If Todd Orlando set a table the way he coached Texas to set the edge, all of Grandma's china would be thrown at the guests from 20 yards away. The Horns were the second most penalized defense in the league, the least fundamentally sound, and objectively one of the most underachieving units in recent Longhorn memory.

"You know, a football coach is nothing more than a teacher. You teach them the same subject, and you have a new group of guys every year." - Darrell K Royal

DKR's wisdom rings true even more with every passing year. So too do the lessons of the great John Wooden. Wooden, architect of the greatest college basketball dynasty ever (with the help of a generous booster or two), began the first practice of each year the same way. He brought the entire team around him and then methodically demonstrated how to properly put on socks and shoes. True story. The most respected coach of his era, perhaps ever, began the first team practice focused on blister avoidance and how to tie one's shoes to ensure maximal support. Every year. Even with the squads that won ten national championships between 1964-1975. Imagine that level of commitment to process

and foundational concepts when every human instinct is to think: "Look, we got this" and "this is now beneath me."

Perhaps that is why it is Wooden's Pyramid of Success, not Wooden's Inverted Tetrahedron of Some Plays I Drew Up. As DKR reminds us, you have a new group of guys every year. Wooden's symbolic message was the same: there would be no assumptions made about anyone's knowledge level. The fundamentals of the game would be taught patiently and correctly. Starting with shoes. Then how to properly set a screen. Perform a bounce pass. Feed the post. The theory of attacking a 2-3 zone would not come until a baseline of common aptitudes had been established, taught, and nurtured. It is easy to have sympathy for the UCLA senior repeat national champion enduring a sock lecture, but how easy is it to be the championship coach humbling himself for the third decade in a row teaching the exact same fundamentals? The man had coached eighteen teams to Final Four appearances. And there he was, on his knees, putting socks and shoes on a player the Bruin way.

As a great professor once remarked,"I have to remind myself that these young students making the same damn mistakes every year are actually different students making new mistakes to them. They are only the same mistakes to me."

The Longhorn defensive staff failed to teach foundational knowledge or basic principles of the game, so they resorted to exerting control. A poor tactical solution to a fundamental strategic failure to teach the game. If there was one moment emblematic of the 2019 Longhorn season, it came on 3rd and 17 against eventual national champion LSU, before a fired up Texas home crowd. With 2:38 on the clock, and the Texas offense dominating (the Horns scored on every 2nd half possession), down 37-31, LSU ball on their 39 yard line, Todd Orlando chose to go with a zero blitz on the game's most important play. He could not trust players he had not taught or granted agency to exercise their judgement in a more situational defense. Texas brought six men, leaving four Texas defensive backs in single coverage on four LSU receivers (the middle safety, Chris Brown, did not have depth and was a quarterback spy - effectively caught in no-man's land). Anticipating the pressure, LSU quarterback Joe Burrow evaded the blitz and threw the game-sealing 61 yard touchdown pass to LSU slot receiver Justin Jefferson.

The call was symbolic of the season and Todd Orlando's rise and fall at Texas. It also defied Football 101. It was bad probability analysis. The nonsensical logic of hitting on 18 because the dealer won't expect it. It also ignores the larger context of the game. All that matters in that situation is possession of the ball. A 10-yard gain on 3rd and 17 is cause for riotous celebration. You do not double down on a failed tactic that will surrender 470 passing yards, while placing your secondary in single coverage against a cadre of NFL first round draft picks.

It was a useful encapsulation of Todd Orlando's 3rd down problem because it occurred again and again throughout the 2018 and 2019 seasons. In 2018, the Longhorns ranked 9th of 10 Big 12 teams in 3rd down defense. In 2019, they finished 6th. Collectively ranking in the bottom quartile of a league not known for its defensive prowess over a two season 18 game sample size is more than just bad luck. A consistent failure on money downs is either a talent problem, a coaching problem, or both. The Texas defense does not have a talent problem. Texas has (or had) a coaching and developed talent problem. Increasingly, the Texas defense became just a bunch of calls on a play sheet. Lame, laminated attempts to outguess the opposing offense.

The fallacy of an overly orchestrated defense is roughly the equivalent of walking into a strip mall martial arts studio only to be greeted by a man in a black robe with a flaming tiger stenciled on it. The man - a Master!- informs you that if you will throw a punch at him at exactly the speed (very slow, with the hand he tells you), timing (when he says), and precise angle (one that does not occur in a fight) he requires, he will block it in a stylish way punctuated by a loud cry, setting off a chain of amazing techniques that will end with you on the floor and your beating heart in his hand. Meanwhile, a Big 12 conference full of spread offense mixed martial artists, popping gum and wearing flip-flops, stroll into the dojo, take up his challenge, disinterestedly double leg him to the ground, get mount, and render corrective noogies until he can name five kinds of breakfast cereal.

Football is not a whiteboard kata.

A defense is eleven men in a bad mood playing their positions and doing their jobs within a larger construct. That construct is the scheme, but the scheme does not exist on an ethereal white board. It exists within each player's understanding of their role. Some players have necessarily narrow assignments. Hedgehogs. Other positions (safety, nickel, linebacker - at minimum) require individual agency if you want a successful defense. Some aspects of the defense must be open-ended: agile, facile, flexible, capable of course correction. The way to combat wide open offense is teaching defensive players the overarching principles and precepts of the game, thus giving them the ability to react to what they see with a clear mind and fast legs. It's teaching position-unit-scheme. Reverse that order at your peril. Remove the first step or two entirely? Get a good realtor.

Ever wonder why the Orlando defense could cross train its linebackers and defensive backs so easily at every position? Because they were not learning a position, they were just memorizing a call. If you understand that difference, you understand everything.

Texas should field a top tier defense in the league every year. That is a reasonable *minimal* expectation. A failure to meet that standard is a coaching failure in recruiting, development, scheme, or basic teaching.

Texas must teach from the position level up. That is why Chris Ash is in Austin. To teach. To take on the task that DKR and Wooden and other great teachers fundamentally understand. Ash is a back-to-basics instructor and a documented fixer. And his fixes at Ohio State helped lead directly to a national title. In 2014, Ash took over a blistered Buckeye defense that ranked 57th in the country by DFEI metrics. They were particularly terrible against the pass and known for poor tackling and fundamentals. They also had pretty good, but underachieving, athletes. A year later, the 2015 Buckeye defense finished their national championship run ranked 13th in the country. Up 44 spots from 2014. With seven returning defensive starters, Ash took Ohio State up to 7th in the country in 2015. That is certainly the trend line that Texas fans are looking for. Fortunately, Ash's track record does not suggest a one hit wonder whose ship may have been raised by random tides of talent. At Wisconsin in 2011, Ash's first year ever as a defensive coordinator, the Badgers were ranked 48th nationally in defense. A year later, they were ranked 18th, up 30 spots. At every stop the feedback is the same: great defensive back coach, good fundamentals, constant drill on basics, sound teaching. The criticisms, if more muted, are also the same: simplicity can become predictability and a lack of exposure to innovative offenses.

Whether that means Ash is an upgraded Greg Robinson or the next Will Muschamp remains to be seen. We know that the 2020 defensive staff will have a massive basic teaching deficit to overcome. If that deficit is not addressed, Ash's scheme will fail as it relies so heavily on fundamentals and individual player agency. The Longhorns need to get coached up and smartened up. That will take a little time. As for Ash's time coaching at Rutgers? Forget Rutgers. Ash going 8-32 as a head coach for the Scarlet Knights is irrelevant. There are plenty of head coaching failures who are terrific coordinators. Ash's most important traits will be demonstrated by his ability to guide his positional hires in how he wants the game taught, his own ability to coach a position, his understanding of the challenges posed by Big 12 schematic diversity, and his overall ability to enforce a standard of play. The Texas defense will turn it around by teaching the game of football within a sane scheme. By deploying its best players in the proper positions. By demonstrating basic competence in development. Deprived of spring practices, Texas will have to do much of its teaching on the fly during the course of the season. The open date after UTEP and before Kansas State will be an instructional gold mine for applying the lessons learned from the first three contests.

Schematically, Chris Ash historically prefers four-man fronts backed by quarters coverage in a 4-2-5 alignment. The simplicity of quarters concepts - four defensive backs and three linebackers (one is the Spur, effectively a nickel) in zones - belies its open-ended rules to counter an offense. Each individual defender must learn to read keys, which tell them where their responsibilities rest. Responsibilities ranging from single coverage, run support, passing off receivers, bracketed combinations, and the calculated gamble of jumping a route. It is a zone defense operating under man-to-man principles (often called man-under) that allows the defense to opportunistically double team the offense's #1 wide receiver or send help where needed. Robots cannot play in it because it operates on principles. It requires

instinctive athletes, operating on larger concepts than "stand there, now run there" guidance. The philosophy is also sound against the run as it gives clear responsibilities in run support and it can bring up extra men from multiple spots. The defense, like all defenses, has flaws. For example, if the cornerbacks cannot play man coverage successfully outside the hashes knowing that they typically have help inside, things can get ugly. Also, if the nickel (Spur) and the safety behind him cannot handle the slot receiver (typically, on short routes, the Spur has him; if he runs deep, he passes to the safety) go ahead and strike up the wrong marching band. Linebackers must be able to diagnose, attack downhill, and play off of the ball. Safeties must be smart, instinctive, and can't second-guess what they see unfolding in front of them. Cornerbacks have to possess short memories, the ability to play the ball in the air, and the press skills to disarm timing routes. The defensive line must get pressure with four rushers and hold the edge in the running game.

While Texas has a good personnel fit for any front, it is important to deploy athletes like Ossai, Ojomo, and Coburn correctly. Odd versus even front debates are reductive. Those advancing that three man fronts under Orlando as the primary cause of failure should consider that Baylor, the best defense in the conference in 2019, ran a base three man front, with the best pressure and sack rate in the Big 12. They just did it very differently (i.e. correctly) from Texas. However, this Texas personnel group is particularly well-suited to a four-man front. So, let's talk about the big nasties.

Defensive Line

99	**Keondre Coburn** 26 TACKLES, 4.5 TFL, 2 SACKS	6-2	350	Sophomore (RS)
49	**Ta'quon Graham** 31 TACKLES, 12 TFL, 3.5 SACKS	6-3	295	Senior
98	**Moro Ojomo** 13 TACKLES, 2.5 TFL	6-2	285	Sophomore (RS)
93	**T'Vondre Sweat** 9 TACKLES, 1 TFL, 1 SACK	6-3	335	Sophomore
42	**Marqez Bimage** 12 TACKLES, 2 TFL, 1 SACK	6-2	270	Senior
36	**Jacoby Jones** 14 TACKLES	6-3	265	Senior
88	**Daniel Carson**	6-4	310	Sophomore (RS)
92	**Myron Warren**	6-3	290	Freshman (RS)
	Peter Mpagi	6-4	310	Freshman (RS)
81	**Reese Leitao**	6-3	290	Junior
48	**Vernon Broughton**	6-4	295	Freshman

	Alfred Collins	6-5	285	Freshman
91	Sawyer Goram-Welch	6-4	280	Freshman

Keondre Coburn is the unquestioned starter at nose tackle and the 350-pound 1 technique (shaded shoulder of the center) should be even more of a handful playing in an attacking four-man line. The sophomore has 12 career starts and his play steadily improved over the course of the year. An interior defender Coburn's size profiles as a dormant space eater to the casual analyst, but film study reveals something very different: Coburn is a line of scrimmage altering penetrator. Size does not make Coburn special - it is his quickness *at that size*.

The key is keeping Keondre's snap count reasonable so that his big motor can rev in spurts rather than overplaying him and seeing his gas tank come up empty at the end of drives or in the fourth quarter. Oscar Giles and Chris Ash know that Coburn playing 45 maniacal

snaps will create better total outcomes than the accumulated fatigue of an every-down player. Given the depth on the Longhorn defensive line, finding effective relief poses little problem. Crucially, Coburn will also get some significant schematic help. The front will be coached to practice such controversial junior high principles as "containment" and "edge setting" so that Coburn's interior penetration in the passing and running game will be rewarded with tackles for loss instead of the running back squirting around the unprotected edge, or a quarterback casually rolling away from pressure to throw a strike downfield. On review, the prospectus counted 5 tackles for loss and at least 1 sack that Coburn was cheated during the course of the 2019 season due to this simple schematic failure. Coburn is a handful for any center and despite his size he has a drag racer's first step and a high work rate. Combine that with a low center of gravity and a rhino's lower body strength and the physics get interesting for whatever is standing in front of him. His impact may not always show up in the box score, but to the discerning eye, it should be written all over the field.

Ta'Quon Graham was not well served by last year's scheme, but he was quietly ranked second on the team in tackles for loss (12.0) and sacks (3.5). Graham showed his ability to disrupt against Utah after new management let the defensive line dogs out of the kennel and Ta'Quon notched 2.5 tackles for loss and a sack in that contest. Graham is an experienced defensive lineman with 15 career starts and 39 career appearances, but he has largely been to date a solid cog in a defense that did little to feature his potential impact. This season is his opportunity to break out and show out for the NFL draft. He will do so largely playing inside as a 3 technique (the area on the outside shoulder of the guard) which is a favorable place for a penetrating lineman to shoot gaps and generally be a disruptive pain. Lining up next to Keondre Coburn with Joseph Ossai outside is not a bad place to find opportunity for an enterprising defensive lineman. Graham has solid quickness for his size, but he is not in the special category. However, he can be explosive through contact, has the requisite physicality to fight a double team, and has exhibited a high motor against the running game. As a pass rusher, Graham has a tendency to stop at resistance, watch the quarterback, and try for opportunistic tipped balls. That will simply not be allowed in this new defense and the Utah bowl game suggests that this is a habit Graham can break.

Moro Ojomo wisely redshirted as a freshman and saw quality snaps last year, including starts against Kansas and Texas Tech. Ojomo graded well in his limited action at defensive end and nose tackle and was particularly effective in his rotation snaps against Kansas State,

Oklahoma State and Utah. So why didn't we see Moro of Ojomo? It is a fair question and the new defensive philosophy should play to some of his strengths. Ojomo will primarily play 3 technique but he is versatile enough to help out at strong side defensive end or even as a 1 technique in a predictable passing situation. That versatility will allow him to serve as a utility player, capable of pitching in wherever needed. Once he learns to use his hands and leverage better and not get big-brothered by taller offensive linemen with longer wingspan, Ojomo can be a potential plus pass rusher. Ojomo is young for his class having started his schooling at age 4 in Lagos, Nigeria, so remain patient with his development. At minimum, Moro will be a significant rotation asset.

Any notions that **T'Vondre Sweat** would be redshirting began to dissipate on reporting day when Texas coaches saw Sweat's maturation, a belief later confirmed when

the pads came on. The former Huntsville defensive end now weighs 0.96 Coburns and quickly asserted himself as Keondre's primary back-up on the inside. Sweat participated in all 13 Longhorn contests last year and played consistently well given his inexperience. Now a sophomore, Sweat will continue to be Coburn's primary back-up and may even share the field with Coburn in certain short yardage or goal line situations. Getting some push on a combined 685 angry interior pounds on 3rd and 1 won't be an easy task. While the widespread distribution of spread passing offenses does not much favor the concept of a gigantic nose tackle run stopper trying to get sustained pass rush over four quarters, massive interior players with high motors, an actual ability to rush the passer, and the opportunity to rest each other in a relentless tag team can still make for a potent combination. Sweat will do a fine job of resetting the line of scrimmage in the Longhorn's favor. A fair comparison to his game would be Chris Nelson: strong as a bull, active, but not as disruptive as the Poona Ford/Keondre Coburn school of bursty big guys.

Marqez Bimage is a high effort former linebacker with 34 game appearances in his Longhorn career. Prior defensive philosophy featured him inside, counting on his strength and quickness to offset his size disadvantages. He was a reasonable contributor, but like many of his defensive line peers, he had only sporadic opportunity to highlight his ability. In the new scheme, the senior will compete for the starting role at strong side defensive end, where he will continue to be asked to hold the line of scrimmage and still see some snaps inside, but he will receive far more opportunities to attack gaps and battle offensive tackles in space, particularly on clear passing downs. Bimage is plenty strong - he boasts a nearly 700-pound squat - but his ability to excel outside will be predicated on his quickness, pass rushing ability, and skill set. Bimage will be locked in a battle at strongside defensive end beyond just August camp. Given a wealth of resources, Texas will not be content at any of the defensive line positions if they are not getting the desired impact. Given the diverse three-deep at the position, Longhorn defensive ends understand that their job security is purely performance based.

Strongside defensive end **Jacoby Jones** came to Austin by way of Butler Community College in Kansas. He contributed 14 tackles in spot action last year, but without the requisite size and strength to play the interior 4i position, he was an underutilized asset. The senior now finds himself in a defense that plays more to his strengths. Jones is a potential difference maker for his pass rushing ability. Jacoby does not possess particularly overwhelming physical attributes, but he has a solid first step, plays with anticipation, can cover ground, and does a nice job swatting away hands while taking efficient angles to the quarterback. At minimum, Jones should have been tried as a specialist pass rushing asset for a Texas defense that struggled to get honest pressure (and dishonest pressure). Jacoby has a good feel for space and angles in T/E stunts (the interior lineman crashes the outside gap, creating conflicted assignments for blockers, while the end loops inside through vacated space) and it will be interesting to see what the senior is capable of under live fire. If he can be a difference maker rushing the passer on situational downs with Joe Ossai lined up on the other Ossaide, the defensive pass rush will be hard to deal with.

Daniel Carson, a once lithe 235 pounder, has responded to the weight room and training table to add more than fifty pounds to his frame. Carson is learning the new levers of his big body and in an interior defensive room packed with talent, the third-year interior defender and former high school basketball and track standout will have to show considerable growth to earn a spot in the rotation. When a solid athlete of Carson's background struggles to find the field, it is a good sign of a positional talent level on the rise.

Myron Warren took a much-needed redshirt last year and the former 240-pound tomahawk dunking high school edge rusher emerged from Yancy McKnight's S&C program as a 290 pounder. Like fellow Louisianian Malcolm Roach, if Warren retains his dexterous athletic attributes in his new body, he could be a very interesting value proposition on the interior or exterior defensive line. It is not surprising that an athlete who hails from a town called Many could have several future uses.

Reese Leitao was moved from tight end to defense to better distribute practice snaps to the youngsters in the tight end room.

Peter Mpagi has been diagnosed with a heart condition and will not play in 2020. We wish him the very best.

Vernon Broughton and **Alfred Collins** are extremely talented incoming freshman defensive linemen who possess the size, maturity, and ability to earn instant playing time. However, Texas has the enviable problem of a solid depth chart. Longhorn coaches expect one of both of them to play, but that privilege will have to be earned competing against some good older players. Both Broughton and Collins could play strongside defensive end or three technique, but size, need, and affinity will determine that soon enough. Speaking of size, Collins weighed in at 247 pounds in March, 2019. Nine months later, he was a very well put together 285. Fellow lineman **Sawyer Gorham-Welch** was an opportunistic late take from Longview. Expect him to redshirt.

Prognosis

The 2019 defensive line was so fundamentally mismanaged at the schematic level that many Longhorn faithful began to question if Texas even had good players. Texas had and still has good players on the defensive line. In fact, Texas now has more of them. When those good players were allowed to play winning football in the bowl game against Utah, they dominated a highly productive Ute offense, thoroughly owning the line of scrimmage for four quarters. An unrelenting rotation of Coburn, Graham, Ojomo, Roach and Sweat yielded sixteen tackles, six tackles for loss, two sacks, batted balls, and multiple quarterback hits while completely stoning the Ute power running game and owning short yardage situations. While Utah's relatively conventional offense was ripe for exploitation, the Longhorns never showed that kind of domination against comparable season opponents. Four of those Longhorn defensive linemen return and in addition to their own individual improvement, they will be supplemented by veterans recast in better spots and some brilliant young talent.

It was a frustrating season trying to convince Texas fans that the defensive line was a much more talented unit than the Longhorn staff schemed them to be. In 2020, Texas will be able to show what talented athletes can do when the defense sets the edge (controlling the outside shoulder of the most exterior blockers and constricting space, while preventing a bounce out with the defender's outside shoulder free), establishes containment (the pass rushing version of setting the edge, compressing the pocket and disallowing quarterback bail outs), and stops making defensive linemen take lateral steps after the snap. The Texas defensive line is good. And if some players pan out at the strongside defensive end position,

creating a fearsome foursome with the JACK linebacker, backed up by a strong rotation that goes nearly three-deep? Look out.

Position Coach

Oscar Giles returned to Texas after a combined 15 years combined as a player (1987-1990) and coach (defensive ends, 2005-2013, 2017) in Austin. The esteemed Recruiterati (like the Illuminati but powerless and possessed of unhealthy obsessions with 17-year olds) consider Giles an average recruiter at a position group where many programs house their heaviest hitters. Giles will coach the defensive ends in 2020.

Mark Hagen will join Oscar Giles on the defensive line staff to coach the interior, giving the Longhorns a lot of opportunity to maximize an already high-level talent base. 24 of Hagen's 28 years in coaching have been in the SEC or Big 10. Hagen has stops at Indiana, Texas A&M and Purdue, but his recruiting ability is unknown.

Linebacker

46	**Joseph Ossai**	6-4	250	Junior
	90 TACKLES, 13.5 TFL, 5 SACKS, 2 INT			
50	**Byron Vaughns**	6-4	240	Sophomore (RS)
	14 TACKLES			
40	**Ayodele Adeoye**	6-0	250	Sophomore (RS)
	45 TACKLES, 3 TFL, 2.5 SACKS			
6	**Juwan Mitchell**	6-1	240	Junior
	39 TACKLES, 3.5 TFL, 3 SACKS			
33	**David Gbenda**	6-0	225	Freshman
31	**Demarvion Overshown**	6-3	215	Sophomore (RS)
	18 TACKLES, 7 TFL, 2 SACKS			
13	**Marcus Tillman**	6-1	235	Freshman
44	**Tyler Owens**	6-2	210	Senior
	Jaylan Ford	6-2	210	Freshman
	Prince Dorbah	6-2	215	Freshman
	Jaden Hullaby	6-2	210	Freshman

Junior **Joseph Ossai** is a potentially dominant edge player waiting for a coaching staff to notice. Rather than build on his terrific Sugar Bowl game performance against Georgia as a true freshman playing on the line of scrimmage where he led the Horns' defense in tackles, the Texas brain trust looked at the tall natural pass rusher with a relentless motor and mused,"I bet he could cover the flat so we can blitz our deepest safety." Ossai can do that. But just because a player *can*, doesn't mean

a player *should*. They probably would have played Lawrence Taylor at fullback.

Despite the schematic wizardry that took a predatory lion and tried to turn him into a deliberative housecat, Ossai still performed. As a sophomore, despite wearing a shoulder sling to stabilize a separated shoulder and pinched nerve for most of the season, grossly miscast in Todd Orlando's defense as a predominantly off-of-the ball and coverage linebacker, Ossai still shined through as the best player on the Longhorn defense. Joseph led the team in tackles (90), tackles for loss (13.5), sacks (5), had nine quarterback hits (the next best Longhorn defender had three), added two interceptions (2nd on the team), had as many pass break-ups as free safety Caden Sterns, and forced a fumble. Those numbers were substantially buoyed by the only game where he was deployed correctly by an interim staff: the Alamo Bowl against Utah. There he registered nine tackles, six tackles for loss, and three sacks. Godzilla left smaller paths of destruction through Tokyo than Ossai did in San Antonio against the overmatched Utes. Now with 15 starts under his belt and a new staff's guidance, his 2020 prospects are bright if this staff can piece together the commonalities of Ossai's dominating bowl performances.

Ossai is a talented, intelligent, hard-working athlete begging for a scheme that will play him correctly as an edge setter, pass rusher, and general disruptor. Chris Ash will see to that with Ossai's deployment at the JACK position - a hybrid linebacker/defensive end role that will play Joseph on the line of scrimmage, standing up or with a hand down, with the primary task and purpose of getting after the passer and setting the edge in the run game. Due to his quickness and effort level, he will also be disruptive from the backside when teams try to run away from him. Ossai will still occasionally drop into coverage - and should do so, as he is excellent at it - but that will be a change-up, not a primary role. A necessary off-speed pitch to make the fastball of Longhorn pressure more unpredictable. Joe Ossai is a high NFL draft pick waiting to happen with the requisite athletic

character to drag the Texas defense back to winning prosperity. To abet that, the Texas defensive staff needs to lead, follow, or get out of his way.

Ayodele Adeoye led the inside linebackers in tackles (45) while starting ten games for the Longhorns. Frankly, film review does him few favors when offenses offer misdirection or put him into conflict, but it is also difficult to account for how he was coached and the effects of a failed scheme that turned every inside linebacker into a default, obvious blitzer. The powerfully built inside linebacker looks like a starting NFL player in pads and was highly recruited out of high school, but his 245-pound frame and perceived lack of mobility is a departure from the current model of linebacker that thrives best in the Big 12. That written, Adeoye did have a fine interception against West Virginia and has shown some ability to drop into zones and break up passes, though he is not an ideal candidate for man coverage on a running back. The physical third year sophomore will compete for a starting job inside.

Marcus Tillman was an early enrollee freshman who redshirted after sustaining a knee injury against Oklahoma State. The former Florida high school safety has filled out and looks like a linebacker now. It is possible that the inexperienced Tillman could provide a different and much more athletic option at Mike linebacker competing against Mitchell and Adeoye. He came to Texas as a position switch and already sushi raw, so that is an optimistic projection for a redshirt freshman. Texas coaches like Tillman and expect him to be a contributor. The only question is when.

Last year, the prospectus argued that safety **DeMarvion Overshown** should be moved to linebacker. He did not move to linebacker. This year, the new Texas defensive staff will move Overshown to linebacker. Whether Overshown knows that yet depends on when you are reading this preview. Despite seeing game action in a mere eight contests and notching only two starts, Overshown finished the year with seven tackles for loss, good enough for 4th on the entire Texas defense. He also notched two sacks, a forced fumble, three pass break-ups, an interception, and a quarterback hit. Overshown fills up the box score and stopping Big 12 offenses demands linebacking multi-tools capable of doing exactly that. His ratio of game impact to participation speaks to Overshown's elite quickness and God-given ability to explode in any direction. Utter fearlessness also plays a role and Overshown has added weight to his lean frame to aid durability, but still runs as quickly laterally as he does in a straight line. The Texas defense badly needs to increase its speed and quickness at linebacker and Overshown's potential ability to cover in space and eliminate running game angles is a needed ingredient for the Texas defense to ascend to its full potential against spread offenses. Overshown struggled with ankle, neck, and back injuries last year, in no small part because of his kamikaze play style, so that should also factor into his best employment. Overshown will not be a studied or particularly fundamental linebacker - his game is about twitch, instinctive reaction, and running

down rabbits like a greyhound. He will blow assignments, fly through the wrong gap, and learn some hard lessons in real time. The juice will be worth the squeeze if the Texas defensive staff creates a role that allows him to see-ball, chase-ball as much as possible.

Byron Vaughns will back up Joseph Ossai as the JACK linebacker and the redshirt sophomore has plenty of athletic traits to fall in love with. His biggest contribution of the year came against Kansas, where Vaughns registered eight tackles as six Longhorn starters succumbed to injury or suspension. Vaughns came to Austin as a skinny 200-pound linebacker/wide receiver and has transformed his body in short order with the help of Yancy McKnight and a redshirt season. Expect Vaughns to back-up Ossai and if he can put together a sufficiently impressive August, perhaps even find his way onto the field on clear passing downs as an additional pass rusher. Vaughns was suspended for the Alamo Bowl for a team infraction, but it served as a growth opportunity and is not a concern.

Juwan Mitchell earned five starts and played in eleven games, totaling 39 tackles, three sacks and four pass break ups at inside linebacker. The mercurial New Jersey native revealed himself to be a very physical player - his desire for contact is not an issue - but he was too often caught flat-footed watching the play develop when not employed as a run blitzer. In fact, his most productive use was largely crashing into the A gap. A bit predictable, but stuff got moved around sometimes. Nor did he show consistently good technique when taking on or attempting to shed blockers. The late 2019 JUCO signee from Butler Community College is still only a junior, so improvement under a new defensive regime is still possible. When his head is right, Mitchell is capable of playing effectively for Texas, but he needs active, disruptive defensive linemen up front and to be surrounded by speed on the back end to relieve him of disadvantageous coverage and pursuit assignments.

David Gbenda is an undersized linebacker with good range who could provide depth at weak side or middle linebacker. He even briefly moved to running back out of desperation as the Longhorn depth chart winnowed down to uncomfortably thin levels. Now he is back at his natural position. Gbenda played sparingly last year to preserve his redshirt and fits the mold of the new spread-busting linebacker archetype. Fitting a mold and being good enough are separate ideas and it is up to Gbenda to impress enough to push for a spot on the two-deep. Like Byron Vaughns, he was suspended from the Alamo Bowl for breaking a rule, but that incident is a non-factor.

Tyler Owens was moved to linebacker from safety in an attempt to get more speed at the position. Given that Owens is one of the fastest players on the team (he logged a 10.29 100 meters in high school) he brings that attribute in spades. As a freshman, Owens' athleticism demanded inclusion on the Longhorn special teams and he saw spot game action as well. He is on a steep curve of development given that Owens was a late-developing star where the switch turned on in his senior season,

transforming him from a great athlete playing football to a football player who is also a great athlete. It will be a challenge for the sophomore to further demonstrate his adaptability and to apply his elite athleticism on the field at a novel position.

Prince Dorbah, **Jaylan Ford** and **Jaden Hullaby** should all earn redshirts unless injuries or off-season woes afflict the depth chart.

Walk-on linebackers **Cort Jaquess**, **Luke Brockermeyer**, **Jett Bush**, and **Jake Ehlinger** form the most talented group of non-scholarship players on the roster. Cort Jaquess impressed the staff enough to start the first half of the Alamo Bowl and he notched five physical tackles, performing at a level indistinguishable from Adeoye and Mitchell at Mike linebacker. While the thought of relying on walk-ons to improve the Texas depth chart might be disconcerting to some, those players provide a solid positional floor and the prospect cannot be dismissed out of hand. Every now and then a program strikes gold on Clay Matthews, Aeneas Williams, JJ Watt, Carl Nassib, Jordy Nelson, or Antonio Brown. All of those NFL stars were former walk-ons. The odds of that increase substantially the higher the baseline quality of preferred walk-on. Likely? No. But why not help your odds with a robust walk-on program? Texas has done that and Herman should be applauded for that part of the program.

Prognosis

The key to this unit's maximization will be in the proper allocation of resources, the appropriate matching of task to ability, and the development of the athletes brought in to transform the unit into a more dynamic entity.

First, allocation. Joseph Ossai is an edge-defending hybrid linebacker pass rusher who must be deployed as such. That just improved the Texas defense markedly. DeMarvion Overshown is an off-the-ball linebacker who must be placed in a role that allows him to run, attack, cover and play instinctively as a ball chaser, protected from blockers. With that, team speed, aggression, and off-schedule dynamic play potential just got better. Similarly, Tyler Owens to linebacker was a smart move, but that bet may not hit immediately. Should Overshown falter in that role , B.J. Foster deserves a tryout.

Second, matching task to ability. The most experienced Mike linebackers - Mitchell, Adeoye, Jaquess - are best as interior run stoppers. The scheme must be built with that in mind. Their responsibilities must be winnowed down to a mission set that they can accomplish. Crucially, all three must be better tutored at performing that interior role better. Just because that is what they do best does not mean that they are operating at a high standard. Marcus Tillman represents a different type of inside linebacker, but absent August practices, we cannot yet gauge his readiness.

Third, quickly progressing dynamic athletes like Overshown, Owens, and Tillman is crucial to the defense becoming a top 25 unit. That is not easy and it is a dual task for both Hutzler and Ash. The linebacker coach has to teach the basics to what amounts to three converted safeties, while Ash needs to coordinate the defense with an understanding of those player's strengths and deficiencies. Broadly speaking, if Texas cannot find ways to get positionless players like B.J. Foster or Overshown opportunity in a college football universe where aggression and quickness are the ultimate currency, it might tell us as much about the limitations of the coaches as the players.

Position Coach

Coleman Hutzler sounds like the name of a SAE who still owes you money from a college ski trip, but the new linebacker coach will be a significant upgrade for Texas. He spent the last four seasons at South Carolina learning from Will Muschamp (he also coached with him at Florida) and, like tight end coach Jay Boulware, he has high level special teams coordinator experience. Before South Carolina, Hutzler spent time coaching linebackers at Boston College, a place with a pretty solid, hard-nosed linebacking tradition of its own. Prior to that Hutzler was at Florida, where he also coached linebackers and special teams. Hutzler is considered a hustler: an up and coming star, a recruiting asset, and a bright enough football light to help Chris Ash with game planning.

Cornerback

3	Jalen Green	6-1	195	Junior
	30 TACKLES, 2 INT			
5	D'shawn Jamison	5-10	180	Junior
	35 TACKLES, 3.5 TFL, 3 INT			
29	Josh Thompson	6-0	200	Junior (RS)
	12 TACKLES, 1.5 TFL			
2	Kenyatta Watson	6-1	195	Freshman (RS)
	6 TACKLES			
38	Kobe Boyce	6-0	185	Junior (RS)
	6 TACKLES			
24	Marques Caldwell	6-0	195	Freshman (RS)
	Jahdae Barron	5-11	175	Freshman
	Kitan Crawford	5-11	195	Freshman

Jalen Green has played in 21 career games, recording all seven of his starts in 2019. He totaled 30 tackles with five pass break ups before sustaining a badly dislocated shoulder on a hard tackle against Oklahoma State. Green returned, played through injury, and performed pretty solidly down the back stretch of the season despite several games where he was less than 100%. Unfortunately, like many of his peers, Green suffered from poor position coaching and a larger scheme that did little to develop his skill set so it is difficult to project his true potential absent better teaching on how to line up, use his hands, pattern match routes, or play press coverage. Green brings elite quickness, long arms, and surprising grit to the cornerback position. He will compete for a starting cornerback job and the third-year junior should be reasonably expected to take a leap under the tutelage of Jay Valai and Chris Ash. Now a junior, it is time for Green to help fulfill the potential of the 2018 top ranked defensive back class that he headlined.

D'shawn Jamison started the season on the bench, but ended up starting the last nine games and led the team in interceptions with three. Jamison also recorded 35 tackles, three pass break ups, and forced a fumble. When he was finally given punt return duties, he averaged 25.5 yards per return, including a 71 yarder against Utah in the Alamo Bowl. As a kickoff returner he averaged over 30 yards per return, including a 98-yard touchdown against Rice. Recall that as a true freshman, Jamison housed a 90-yard punt return against Kansas State. Perhaps the individual who keeps bringing back kicks for field-flipping gains and touchdowns despite minimal opportunity should be the primary returner? Last year, Jamison demonstrated speed, dexterity, and playmaking that tantalized Longhorn fans, but he also had some very rough moments with blown coverages,

missed assignments, and misplayed balls. Over the course of the season, he showed improvement and cleaned up his mental game, which bodes well for a starting role in 2020. He was particularly skilled at breaking on balls from off coverage and his scintillating one-handed interception against West Virginia was indistinguishable from history's greatest works of art. Now that Jamison has a coaching staff to teach him the game, there is a good chance that his ability to play multiple coverages will improve and he can put up some necessary skill scaffolding around the foundations of his natural ability. Though Jamison has average size and physicality for the position, he possesses elite agility, ball skills, and instincts, in addition to the episodic amnesia that the position demands.

Josh Thompson redshirted as a junior after sustaining a broken foot in the fourth quarter against the Oklahoma State Cowboys. While unfortunate for Josh, that time on ice may just pay off as he has two years of eligibility left to complete with a new defensive staff that believes they have the tools to upgrade a player who has, at times, been perceived as looking the part better than playing it. A new staff with new eyes saw much to like about Thompson and moved him to cornerback, where his size and raw speed fit the press corner attributes that Chris Ash so covets. Thompson has had three starts and 26 game appearances in his Longhorn career, much of that play spotty. He was miscast as a nickel back and struggled with letting receivers over the top and did not seem to fully grasp the run responsibilities of the nickel position (graphically illustrated in the 2018 West Virginia game). Thompson is one of the fastest athletes on the Longhorn team and at 200 pounds is more than strong enough to manhandle big outside receivers at the line of scrimmage. However, his play in coverage has not been instinctive nor particularly encouraging with the ball in the air. Either the Longhorn staff believes they have found a distressed asset that can be easily upgraded and flipped for profit, or they are a bit too in love with physical traits. Either way, Texas has the depth and options at cornerback to make a change if Thompson's repurpose does not serve their purpose. Thompson looks and tests the part. If his on field play matches his specs, the Longhorns are in the enviable position of having as many as four potential starting level cornerbacks.

Kenyatta Watson saw only spot action so he could preserve his redshirt, but the Longhorn staff saw enough of him in practice to know that he could potentially come on at corner to provide excellent depth and a push to the starting cornerbacks. Watson is a long-framed, incredibly twitchy athlete who was tested with a 45-inch vertical leap as a high school senior. Yes, he can jump high, but the reason why is the more subtle takeaway: Watson has extraordinary genetic potential to manifest power quickly. He can recruit more muscle fibers in a more coordinated, rapid way than normal humans. The application of the vertical leap for cornerbacks is a lot more than just challenging a fade route. It means that

his ability to break on the ball, generate dynamic power, and generally react to the ball or receiver is firmly in the freak range. Throw in his frame and long arms and it all just comes down to coaching and development for the Georgia native.

Kobe Boyce enters his fourth year with the Longhorns and he has accumulated six starts in his career to go with 19 game appearances. He earned four starts last season: the first three contests of the season and the final regular season game against Texas Tech. For the season, Boyce managed to tie the team lead for pass break ups (5), but logged only six tackles and managed no other box score metrics. Boyce has very solid athletic traits, but he has struggled with finding the ball in the air and getting muscled at the catch point. At present, the former starting cornerback is now probably the #5 cornerback on the roster. That is encouraging from a roster talent perspective, but somewhat discouraging in the previous staff's ability to properly assess and distribute playing time.

Marques Caldwell redshirted last year and will battle for a coverage team role.

Freshmen **Kitan Crawford** and **Jahdae Barron** are talented youngsters, but will have little opportunity to crack the two deep absent bad program news.

Safety

7	**Caden Sterns**	6-1	205	Junior
	58 TACKLES, 4 TFL			
25	**BJ Foster**	6-2	210	Junior
	34 TACKLES, 4 TFL, 1 INT			
15	**Chris Brown**	5-9	195	Senior (RS)
	46 TACKLES, 3 TFL, 1 INT			
11	**Chris Adimora**	6-1	210	Sophomore
	10 TACKLES			
39	**Montrell Estell**	6-1	200	Junior (RS)
	27 TACKLES, 1 INT			
23	**Xavion Alford**	6-0	185	Freshman
	Jahdae Barron	6-1	190	Freshman

Caden Sterns finished with 58 tackles, 1 sack, 1 pass break up, and no interceptions last year. That relatively impact-free statistical line from a natural coverage safety, even when you factor in some missed starts, tells you all you need to know about how Caden was miscast, spending more time as a delay blitzer from the concession stands than being used as a classic free safety. If those blitzes were any more telegraphed, they would have been in Morse code. Sterns has already started 21 games in his Longhorn career and he is a preseason favorite to win All-Big 12 honors. No athlete will be more pleased to have new defensive coordinator Chris Ash arrive in Austin than Sterns. Ash's defense will give Sterns the freedom to play field safety, get his eyes on the quarterback, and make plays on the ball. Sterns will also benefit from Ash's technical coaching. Caden is an instinctive deep safety with good lateral ability and the skill to win the ball in traffic from sideline to sideline. While everyone loves the classic punishing safety, the rules of modern football, the capriciousness of targeting calls, and the alacrity with which officials throw flags for targeting means that a coverage defender's ability to play the ball, not punish the receiver, is now at a premium. Modern football rewards playing the ball in the air over punishing the receiver on the ground. That is Caden Sterns' game.

From a developmental perspective, Sterns has to exhibit better physicality in the running game and improve as a tackler overall. He has also struggled with durability and missed five starts last season.

B.J. Foster had an injury-plagued sophomore season that trickled into the spring with corrective shoulder surgery on a bad wing that troubled him throughout 2019. He appeared in nine games, starting eight of them, but missed Rice, Oklahoma State, and TCU and was at 70% in several other contests. Foster relishes the contact and dirty work that some defensive backs shy away from. In fact, many have advocated his move to linebacker and that could be a legitimate option,

particularly if some of the new linebacker candidates do not adapt or leave the program. Failing that, B.J. will compete for the starting job at boundary safety with Chris Brown and for the Spur role with Chris Adimora. Foster exhibits outstanding physicality at the point of attack and is a strong blitzer. He is a player you would like to have on the field and the Texas defensive staff will have their work cut out for them creating a scheme that will get their most dynamic players in the mix and free up excess talent at safety. A healthy B.J. Foster is a real asset.

Last year, **Chris Brown** was slated to be the first safety off of the bench. Someone forgot to tell Brown and he went ahead and won a job, starting the first six games of the season before missing a couple with a forearm injury. Brown returned and quickly got back into the mix, serving as one of the most reliable players on the 2019 defense. The 5th year senior is now a veteran with 35 career appearances and 12 starts. He will compete with B.J. Foster for the starting boundary safety job, but he may also be the primary backup for Caden Sterns at field safety. Brown is an easy player to like: fiery, intelligent, a sound tackler, and fearless. While probably the least impressive raw athlete in the safety room, Brown plays with a game speed that belies his actual foot speed and never shies from contact. Whoever comes up seatless in the game of boundary safety musical chairs will be a first man off of the bench at several spots and a hard person to keep off of the field. Brown is a tough-minded asset on a team that needs to raise their collective mental fortitude.

Chris Adimora impressed as a true freshman, living up to this preview's hype as an underestimated recruit to watch. He logged game action in every Texas contest and began to see real snaps late in the season against Texas Tech and Utah. Adimora will compete for the starting job at the Spur position where his physicality and reliable tackling can be exploited as an extra man in the box. Like B.J. Foster, Adimora has a good feel for zone and team coverage concepts, but it remains to be seen how he will hold up against slot receivers in man under coverage. The former wide receiver has natural ball skills and showed the ability to track the ball in the air. Add Adimora to the list of Texas strengths at a deep position.

Montrell Estell is now a 4th year junior who saw quite a bit of game action last season, notching 26 tackles and an interception over 13 game appearances and 2 starts against Oklahoma State and TCU. He was particularly good in his start against the Cowboys, notching multiple solo tackles and a big interception return. Estell is a former high school triple jump champion who struggled with health early in his career at Texas. Montrell had his first full healthy offseason prior to 2019 after filling out his frame in the weight room and it showed with an injury free 2019 season. He should provide a strong contribution to special teams while backing up Caden Sterns at field safety. Estell is versatile enough to pitch in elsewhere if the injury bug bites. He is a fine demonstration of quality depth.

Xavion Alford and **Jerrin Thompson** are promising safety candidates, but they will likely not be needed for immediate playing time.

Prognosis

Last year, the preview touted the safety room as the most talented unit on the Longhorn team. No unit underachieved more. Poor scheme that asked them to support the run or set the edge from the upper deck of I-35, useless deployment as delay blitzers vacating the middle of the field, and a spate of injuries at least in part fostered by poor tackling form, sabotaged the implied production that accompanied that prediction. As for talent, nothing has really changed. The ability level and depth is there. In fact, the position room has only gotten better with the maturation of the unit and the additions of assets like Adimora and the growth of Estell.

Out wide, the loss of Jalen Green for several games did no favors to anyone, but no position suffered as much from poor alignment between coordinator and position coach. Defensive calls did not match the cornerback's alignment and individual technique seemed left to the athlete. At a position where shooting the wrong hand in press coverage, taking a false step, misaligning, or not understanding where the receiver's route leverage is, is akin to just winging it and hoping for the best. Further, it seemed the coaches had failed to allocate the proper playing time (and thus practice snaps) to the unit's best players. Getting the right starters by season's end was only accomplished by injury, game result, and in-season revolt.

From a schematic perspective, Ash and Valai will bring a defensive philosophy that has the potential to dominate conventional offenses and best lower to mid tier spread offenses. The very best spread offenses will have something for Texas and it will be up to Ash to make adjustments to his preferred 4-2-5 quarters coverages. There is no reason to think that he will not, but it may take a lesson or two. The key is for Longhorn fans to not let great be the enemy of good. Texas can improve substantially on the back end by simply casting players correctly into their roles, starting the best players, and upgrading individual positional teaching. Without a spring, the early season may have to serve to work out growing pains, but so be it. When healthy, and if utilized correctly, this is a very talented defensive backfield group that simply needs coaching, reasonable schemes, and individual maximization within a shared team concept. If you are noticing that sentiment is a broken record for each positional unit on the Texas defense, then you have been paying attention.

Position Coach(es)

Jay Valai brings energy and juice to the cornerback room. The Euless, TX native is a strong recruiter and served as Chris Ash's cornerbacks coach at Rutgers. The Ash and Valai connection goes back a ways - Ash was also Valai's position coach at Wisconsin. Valai understands what Ash wants taught at cornerback and he will pay particular attention to building out fundamentals in a unit that sorely needs them. He has a

reputation as a potential recruiting rainmaker. Texas fans would welcome a downpour.

Defensive coordinator **Chris Ash** also has a strong reputation as a defensive backs coach. He will oversee the safeties and that unit will see a real upgrade in teaching. Ash has a reputation for quick coaching turnarounds at Wisconsin, Arkansas, and Ohio State, always starting with the defensive backfield. Ash and his lieutenant, Jay Valai, have another turnaround project in the Longhorns.

Special Teams

The Longhorn special teams were competent in 2019, finishing the season ranked 46th in the nation, roughly comparable to their #44 ranking in 2018. With the added special teams acumen of Longhorn coaches Andre Coleman, Coleman Hutzler, and Jay Boulware added to the mix along with potentially good coverage and kick return personnel, and a pair of returning starting kickers, there is a real opportunity for this unit to make a big leap up the rankings.

Placekicker

Cameron Dicker hit 14 of 18 field goals (77.8%) and was 6 of 9 from 40+ yards. Dicker the kicker also nailed a season long of 57 yards against Rice. He has the leg. Now it is simply a question of improving accuracy inside the 50. He averaged 60.4 yards per kickoff on 78 attempts and had 49 touchbacks (62.8% touchback percentage). Dicker was also 56 of 57 on extra points. All signs point to an even stronger 2020 and likely All-Conference honors. Dicker also put his head in there a couple of times and made two tackles.

Punter

Ryan Bujcevski showed considerable improvement from a rocky 2018 campaign where he averaged less than 40 yards per kick. His 32 punts yielded a 41.7 average before bowing out of the season with a shoulder injury sustained against TCU. Chris Naggar replaced him and had a 39.3 average on 25 punts. Crucially, their collective net average (punt minus return) was 39.1 yards per kick.

A very good number as a function of their average, but a healthy Bujcevski should improve on that number in 2020. Longhorn opponents averaged only 3.33 yards per punt return and were only able to return 9 punts altogether. That speaks to an emphasis on hang time and direction over line drives booted for distance that create good punt return opportunities. Google's spell check capability suggests that Ryan's 32 punts should be changed to 32 pints and given that he is Australian, the algorithm checks out. The same spell check feature recommends that "blitzes" be substituted with "blintzes." That algorithm also checks out. Last year, both blitzes and blintzes were similarly effective when randomly thrown at opponent offenses.

Kicking Coverage/Returns

Opponents averaged 22.5 yards per kick return though the Longhorns gave up a 98-yard touchdown return to Kansas State in Austin. Texas should be able to field an elite coverage team given the bump in team speed over the last three years.

From a punt coverage perspective, Texas had opponents on lockdown. Opposing punt returners combined for 53 yards on 13 returns and a 4.1 average. Their season long was only 14 yards. Longhorn net punting average (punt minus opponent return) was >40 yards per game in 10 of 12 Longhorn contests. That's getting it done.

The Longhorn kick return game improved from 2019, averaging 25 yards per return, but most of that was attributable to D'Shawn Jamison. Jamison averaged 30.6 yards on only 8 returns, including a 98-yard touchdown against Rice.

All punt returners not named D'Shawn averaged 4.1 yards per punt return. Jamison averaged 25.5 yards per punt return on only 4 returns, including a 71-yard sprint against Utah. Jamison also housed a 90-yard touchdown in 2018 against Kansas State that provided the margin of victory.

Prognosis

While the staff certainly values dependability and will not accept turnovers, the kickoff and punt return teams are full of opportunity for a talented roster to find cheap points and swing field position. D'Shawn Jamison is a gifted returner. Let Andre Coleman tutor him on ball security and let him get after it.

Texas has two returning junior starters at kicker and punter with a combined 50 game appearances. Expect improvements from both.

Texas has an excess of potential talent at cornerback and safety with an influx of young speed at linebacker. It should not be hard to fill out the coverage teams.

Similarly, the return team blockers need to get schemed up properly with tough selfless athletes that will seek contact so that D'Shawn Jamison can get on the College Gameday highlights. That is where the special teams coaching acumen of Hutzler, Boulware, and Coleman will come to the fore.

Texas has few excuses not to have top notch special teams play in 2020.

Schedule and Opponents

2019 RECORD	3 YEAR TREND	5 YEAR TREND
4-8	**21-16**	**40-23**

RETURNING STARTERS	OFFENSE	DEFENSE
13	**7**	**6**

Last Meeting: This is the first contest between Texas and South Florida in a much-anticipated battle of who owns the Horns Up symbol?

Overview

The Longhorns and former head coach Charlie Strong were deprived of a potential grudge match when Strong was fired only three years into his five-year contract in Tampa, just as he was in Austin. Strong took over a loaded South Florida program with 16 returning starters from Willie Taggart's 11-2 2016 squad, and he went 10-2 in his first season. When he won the first seven games of 2018, national media "I-told-you-so's" and a few more "Texas-is-a-cesspool" jibes came out. Strong was 17-2 in his first nineteen games and things looked rosy. Then it all wilted. The Bulls promptly lost six in a row, reeling through the back half of 2018, and then utterly collapsed in 2019. Strong went 4-14 over his last eighteen games against a forgiving schedule, with wins coming against the likes of South Carolina State, 2-10 UConn, and a 4-8 East Carolina. Chiding voices quieted and fingers stopped wagging as national media sought the next story to demonstrate their ignorance. Strong's tenure was characterized by organizational miscues, poor preparation, unreflective post game interviews, and on-field management that looked hauntingly familiar to most Texas fans. Those things are all fixable and not hard-wired to the DNA of any program with new coaching, but Strong did not just underperform on the field.

The problem is that Strong, surprisingly, did not recruit particularly well, garnering a reputation for indifference and neglect. South Florida's 2020 recruiting class finished 106th in the country. That should never happen at any FBS program located in Florida that plays its games in a NFL stadium. In 2019, South Florida inked the 77th ranked national class, trailing Florida Atlantic, Marshall, Toledo, and North Texas. How is that even possible? He also offered the parting gift of a NCAA investigation for potential improprieties during his tenure, and a 3-million-dollar buyout for the rest of his contract at a time when the athletic department is badly cash-strapped. The Bulluminati were not pleased. Charlie could not have blown things up better in Tampa than if he had placed former USF alum Jason Pierre-Paul in charge of the team's 4th of July fireworks display. As one sportswriter succinctly characterized Strong's time at the helm of a once regional power program on the rise,"He just burned it all down."

Jeff Scott will try to sweep aside the ashes and build it back up. An A-hire walking into a F level mess, Scott, the former co-offensive coordinator at Clemson, will try to recreate the Dabo Swinney energy and competitive family environment that turned the Tigers from pretender to contender to champion. Las Vegas sets the program 2020 win-total at 4.5 and that is an accurate estimation of their challenge. The long-term future in Tampa is still potentially sunny, but near-term prospects are hurricane weather.

Strengths: DB

South Florida returns an experienced, quality secondary. South Florida cornerback K.J. Sails transferred to South Florida from North Carolina (started 11 games as a Tar Heel sophomore) and was the most consistent defensive bright spot in 2019. Sails is a lithe cornerback (5-11, 175) with elite quickness and good anticipation. In twelve starts for the Bulls, he tallied five takeaways and 42 tackles with nine other passes successfully defended.

Sails should line up on the Longhorns' best pass catcher and, much like Louisiana Tech's Amik Robertson last year, provide a NFL level athletic challenge. Opposite Sails is Mike Hampton, a tall corner with 24 career starts. Free safety Nick Roberts has logged 22 career starts with five interceptions. Bentlee Sanders is the nickel. He goes 5-9, 175 and the junior has 11 career starts of his own. South Florida does not have much size in the defensive backfield, but they are experienced, quick, and capable. This game within a game against the inexperienced Longhorn receivers will be instructive for both the Texas coaches and discerning Longhorn fans in projecting the efficacy of players like Brennan Eagles against higher end cornerback play. Keep your eye on this matchup.

This is a rather qualified strength, but the South Florida overall defense was not a disaster last year, despite the total failure of the Bulls offense to provide them with any support. They finished the year ranked 53rd in FEI, one spot ahead of...Texas. Let us stipulate that Texas had a bit more to work with, but the Bulls are not going to simply prostrate themselves on defense and allow Texas to do whatever it wants. They allowed a respectable 5.4 yards per play and, on average, opponents did not exceed 400 yards per game allowed. The Bulls were best against the pass, yielding less than 200 yards per contest and not allowing many deep completions. The defensive front seven is quick but undersized and Texas staff should expect defensive coordinator Glenn Spencer to utilize that quickness with movement, multiple fronts, and stunts. USF struggled to stop the run though. Opponents averaged 206.8 yards rushing per game, with

Navy gaining 434 yards on the ground and Memphis 325. In all, seven Bulls opponents eclipsed 200+ yards. Up front, they project across thusly: 6-5, 235, 6-1, 290, 6-4, 270, 6-2, 235 and no USF linebacker exceeds 227 pounds. The Bulls can be muscled around at the point of attack. Keep an eye on middle linebacker Antonio Grier. The 220 pounder is undersized, but he can be a handful when blitzing.

Weaknesses: QB, OL, WR, RB

The USF offense was horrendous last year. They finished the season ranked 117th in FEI with one of the least productive passing offenses in FBS football. Starting quarterback Jordan McCloud completed only 54% of his passes and averaged a dink-n-dunking 6.4 yards per attempt. Other South Florida passers attempted 104 throws, completing just more than half of them for 5.8 yards per attempt. South Florida could not get the ball downfield, nor they could effectively execute the short passing game. In four different games, they threw for less than 131 passing yards. In two of those games, they threw for under 100. There is little guarantee that McCloud will keep his job at quarterback, but none of the replacements scream upgrade. The Bulls averaged less than 170 yards passing per game and no Bulls receiver had more than 350 yards receiving. Those same receivers led the AAC in drops. Leading rusher Jordan Cronkrite is gone and 5-5, 180-pound scatback Johnny Ford is moving from wide receiver to replace him. Kelley Joiner will be the change-up option - at 5-9, 175 pounds - or they will go with Oregon transfer Darrian Felix. The

Bulls offense will be coordinated by Charlie Weis Jr. Whether Weis offers them "a decided schematic advantage" against Chris Ash or if he can fill out a pair of Dockers quite like his father remains to be seen, but he has his work cut out for him.

The Bulls offensive line allowed 45 sacks last year, ranking 126th in FBS football. That they return three starters is either good news or bad news, depending on your perspective. Gone also is disastrous offensive coordinator Kerwin Bell, whose neanderthal offensive philosophies set this unit up consistently for failure. While the USF primary running backs (now all departed) averaged over 5 yards per carry against a fairly weak defensive schedule, when one digs deeper, you find outsized production against very bad teams. South Florida had 26 rushing yards against Wisconsin, 54 against SMU, 61 against Temple, and 93 against Georgia Tech. In those four contests, they averaged 9.5 points per game.

Defensive coordinator Glenn Spencer was at Oklahoma State for seven years between 2011-2017 (let go in 2017 by Mike Gundy) and he will have deep familiarity with his former colleague, new Texas offensive coordinator Mike Yurich. Of course, Yurich will have familiarity with Spencer. That may play to the Horns' advantage given that Yurich was not the coordinator who got fired. South Florida depth is poor. Charlie Strong simply stopped recruiting a few months into his tenure, they did not develop well, and they have questionable reserves behind front line starters. That may not come to a head in a season opener, but Austin's 95-degree September temperatures can wear South Florida down if the Texas offense will get after it with respect to tempo and aggression.

Louisiana State University

Ed Orgeron (5th year at LSU)
Etoufee Background

2019 RECORD	3 YEAR TREND	5 YEAR TREND
15-0	**34-7**	**51-10**

RETURNING STARTERS	OFFENSE	DEFENSE
8	**4**	**4**

Last Meeting: The Texas offense played its best game of the year in one of the best college football games of the season, but a furious 4th quarter featuring 39 combined points came up short for the good guys. Texas trailed 20-7 at the half, but refused to be shaken, scoring on every possession in the second half. Ehlinger threw for 401 and totaled five touchdowns, Duvernay nabbed 12 catches for 154 yards, and Brennan Eagles broke 100 yards with a touchdown, but the offensive explosion was all for naught against a brilliant LSU offense that the Texas defense could simply not corral. With 2:27 left in the 4th quarter, and LSU leading 37-31, Texas had LSU 3rd and 17 on their own 39-yard line. After a Texas timeout, the Horns zero blitzed, Joe Burrow evaded the pressure, and threw a touchdown to Justin Jefferson. Anyone who reduces a football game to one play is almost always missing the boat, but that play was emblematic of so much more that would plague Texas throughout the season, eventually leading to a massive staff overhaul. Still, the resilient Horns quickly rallied to cut the deficit back to 7, but it was too little, too late.

Texas just missed out on one of the greatest potential upsets in school history.

Overview

Last year, this book promised Texas fans that LSU would be the best, most talented team on the schedule by a country mile and were legitimate national title contenders, describing the Bayou Bengal roster as ridiculously loaded. Good job, preview. Before dislocating a shoulder patting my own back, it's also worth reminding you that in the same preview, while praising Joe Burrow as a much better quarterback than he was being perceived by Longhorn fans, Burrow was described as a "poor man's Sam Ehlinger." In trying to praise him, he was actually denigrated. Well, can't put the baseball into the stadium lights with every at bat, can you? Imagine what a rich man's Ehlinger would have done to us.

How great was 2019 LSU? Mentioning them among the best college football teams in history is warranted. The

Tigers have the best resume in college football history. Never before has a national champion beaten 5 teams in the AP Final Top 8. In three consecutive weeks, the Tigers decimated SEC East champion Georgia in the SEC title game 37-10, humiliated Big 12 champion OU 63-28 in a playoff game that was not even that close, then took down a strong Clemson squad by 17 points in the national title game. They deserve mention with squads like '95 Nebraska, '01 Miami, and '05 Texas. That was as devastating an offense as you will find at the college level. Best receivers. Best quarterback. Best schemes. By season's end, probably even the best defense. And certainly the best at faking injuries.

Most of all, LSU's national title was a triumph of self-awareness. Ed Orgeron proved that self-awareness is the most underrated attribute for a head coach, much less any leader. Orgeron knows recruiting, evaluating talent, coaching defensive linemen, and motivation. Not much else. His healthy ego allowed him to hire smarter men to run the Xs and Os and influence the culture, even if that meant that Dave Aranda and Joe Brady stole the headlines, got all of the credit for LSU's success, and Orgeron was only perceived as a colorful figurehead. Too many head men worry about their imprint and influence instead of removing barriers from talented staff. Or even worse, won't hire talented staff that threaten them. That is CoordinatorThink and far too many head coaches are mired in it. Orgeron is under no illusions that he would be a good coordinator, so there is no rivalry with his lieutenants; no need to snub them, control them, or have it his way. He uses that self-

knowledge to free himself from ego. That gravel-voiced Cajun is operating on a higher plane of existence.

Recall that three years into his head coaching career, Ed Orgeron was 10-25 and unceremoniously dumped at Ole Miss. A college football punchline. Who would be dumb enough to hire him? Three years into his college playing career, Joe Burrow was the 3rd string quarterback at Ohio State. Recruited over, irrelevant to Ohio State's plans. Burrow transferred to a notable college football offensive wasteland. Their situations changed rather dramatically in Baton Rouge with the hire of Joe Brady while melding with an elite roster. Together, they won the national title. Burrow, the third string transfer, became a record-shattering Heisman winner. Orgeron, the former punchline, could win governor if he felt like it. You would roll your eyes if you saw it in a Hollywood movie. *It doesn't work that way. So unrealistic.* We think we know. But we really don't know.

We do know that LSU was ravaged by the NFL draft. Fourteen picks selected. Five 1st rounders. Only eight returning starters. How will they possibly recover? With a very talented, but inexperienced roster featuring the best cornerback and the best wide receiver in America, that's how. They also added Bo Pelini as their defensive coordinator and NFL veteran Scott Linehan as their passing game coordinator to replace Joe Brady (Carolina Panthers) and Dave Aranda (new head coach at Baylor). Pelini and Linehan are not Aranda and Brady, but they might do in a pinch.

Strengths: DB, DT, WR, TE, Roster talent

Derek Stingley Jr. was probably the best freshman cover cornerback in college football history (apologies to North Carolina's Dre Bly) and if your first reaction to that statement is: "Well, I don't remember Stingley's name being called in the title game against Clemson" - yes, exactly. The 6-1, 195 sophomore athletic freak earned consensus All-American honors while leading the Tigers with six interceptions. By midseason, offenses began targeting his senior comrade, 2nd round draft pick Kristian Fulton, rather than deal with Stingley. Stingley dominated in man-to-man coverage and was more than up to the task against several wide receivers that went high in the NFL draft. Stingley is also LSU's punt returner. Texas must identify and avoid Stingley. This is not the time for prideful challenges. This is a time for respect, even tactical cowardice. A "we are just going to run our stuff and challenge him mindset" would be a bold move...and a dumb one. Safety JaCoby Stevens returns for his senior season. Grant Delpit got the hype and was capable of incredible flashes, but it was Stevens who was LSU's more reliable safety defender from play to play. The only other experienced Tiger defensive back is nickel Kary Vincent, who has 18 career starts. Vincent has a skill set comparable to D'Shawn Jamison in terms of quickness, but he does not exhibit the same anticipation and general ballerness. The Tigers will have a good defensive backfield overall, but there are plenty of places to throw the ball other than at their All-American cornerback.

The LSU interior defensive line is huge, goes three-deep, and is extremely physical. They also have an influx of highly rated freshman and redshirt freshman to fill out their ranks. Bo Pelini will move LSU from a three man to four-man front, giving them the chance to make more plays inside and not just soak up blocks as offensive line sponges. Tyler Shevlin was LSU's most consistent big man and he is poised for a breakout season. He will rotate with Siaki Ika and both men go around 340. Neil Farrell led the defensive line in tackles last year and the highly regarded Glen Logan also returns, looking to fulfill his promised potential. Behind them are three or four highly talented youngsters. LSU will feature the biggest, most physical interior that Texas will see all season. Get them on the move laterally and challenge their conditioning. The Horns will find out quite a bit about their interior offensive line play in Baton Rouge.

Ja'Marr Chase is the best wide receiver in the country. The Biletnikoff Winner led the Tigers in receiving yardage eight times last year (NFL 1st round pick Justin Jefferson led them seven times) and finished with a gaudy 84 catch, 1780-yard, 20 touchdown season. His 21.2 yards per catch average is staggering given that he also caught more than a few screens and dump offs. Chase torched Clemson's NFL cornerbacks with a 221-yard national title game and he slates to be a Top 10 draft pick in 2021. Chase is not a blazer on the stopwatch, but the 6-0, 200 pounder runs through press coverage like it's a mild annoyance, has flypaper hands, wins every downfield ball with a consistency that defies belief, and accelerates out of his route breaks like a Tesla. He is complemented by freak athlete Terrace Marshall. Marshall missed a few games last year, but still finished with 671 yards receiving and 13 touchdowns. At 6-3, 200, he is a big red zone threat and caught a touchdown on 28.3% of his receptions. Marshall can be inconsistent and has struggled with drops at times, but the junior should show more consistency with a year of starts under his belt. Marshall had 6 catches for 123 yards and 2 touchdowns against Texas last year. The third receiver looks to be Tre Palmer, a speedy, shifty player who recorded a 10.42 100 meters in high school. If you think the LSU passing game died with the departure of Burrow, Brady, Moss and Jefferson, understand that the pass catchers are still just as talented. Also consider that LSU returns several established veterans at tight end, like big Brandon Pettigrew (6-7, 255), who will likely take a passing game back seat to 6-5, 250-pound true freshman Arik Gilbert, the #1 tight end prospect in the country. Gilbert is the highest rated tight end in the history of 24/7 composite recruiting rankings. As a flexed receiver, he could be a matchup nightmare.

Weaknesses: OL, LB, DE

LSU replaces 63.6% of their starters from a 15-0 team. Those replacements are largely very talented, but anticipating no drop off is unrealistic and they will have to use an early schedule of UTSA, Texas, Rice, Ole Miss, and Nicholls State to work out the kinks. Athletically, one of those teams is not like the others. Texas needs to exploit Tiger inexperience with a game plan that challenges the Bengal's brains and not just their brawn.

The Longhorn offense will have an opportunity to target a new defensive scheme with brand new personnel at defensive end and all of the starting linebacker positions. The new four-man front will be an adjustment for the Tigers and their current roster is not overrun with natural 4-3 defensive end candidates. That means repurposing former 3-4 outside linebackers and slimming down a few former interior defensive linemen. TK McLendon and Justin Thomas will get the first shot at defensive end, but young freshman BJ Ojulari (6-3, 225) is expected to push for passing down work. Thomas withdrew from school in October, but returned recently somewhat out-of-shape. This is a real potential question mark. Will LSU be able to get four-man pressure or hold the edge? Pelini's defense relies on it.

The Tigers lost every starting linebacker to the NFL Draft. Their replacements will also learn to navigate a new 4-3 look (really, a 4-2-5) that Longhorn fans should recall from Pelini's time at Nebraska. Middle linebacker Damone Clark will have no problems transitioning to his new role (he was LSU's 6th leading tackler coming off of the bench last year) but the outside linebacker roles are up in the air. Former inside linebacker Micah Baskerville should man another spot, while the talented but troubled former 5-star recruit Marcel Brooks, who was being counted on to contribute, entered the transfer portal in late June and will play elsewhere. Texas must make a point of putting this unit - in combination with the defensive ends - into constant conflict in the running and passing game. LSU cannot be powered over and they have too much pure speed to just turn and pitch the ball to the edge and make it a foot race. Texas must add some elements of misdirection with the expectation that LSU's aggressive, inexperienced players learning a new scheme will overextend themselves. Make them pay for it.

The Tigers will start four new faces on the offensive line to go with senior veteran right tackle Austin Deculus. It will not please Texas fans to learn that three are native Texans: the aforementioned Deculus, Ed Ingram, and Chasen Hines. The LSU offensive line is the biggest Texas will see - they average 6-5, 330 from stem to stern - and their goal is to (literally) weigh on defenders in the run game and present an impenetrable interior wall in pass protection. It will be up to Myles Brennan to deal with exterior pressure by getting the ball out quickly to Chase and Marshall. Guard Ed Ingram is not entirely unproven - he started as a true freshman before being suspended for a violation of team rules, losing his job last year. New left tackle Dare Rosenthal backed up Saahdiq Charles last year and word from the swamps is that the former defensive tackle is the most athletic player on the unit and will eventually be a high round NFL draft pick. The LSU offensive line is talented, but they do not have a lot of time working together as a unit and it is not clear how well Linehan and Ensminger (LSU's "official" offensive coordinator) will protect this unit in the same way that

Joe Brady's brilliant play-calling did. They will run block for a talented running back corps featuring John Emery and Chris Curry, tasked to replace the void left by the multi talented Clyde Edwards-Helaire. Watching the pads pop against a talented, physical Longhorn defensive line will be fun.

LSU quarterback Myles Brennan is not a weakness, but compared to Joe Burrow's senior season, well, Brennan has some pretty big shoes to fill. Burrow put together the greatest passing season in college football history, throwing for 5,671 yards and 60 touchdowns while completing around 77% of his passes. All while averaging well over 10 yards per attempt. Brennan has thrown for 600 yards over the course of his career in spot action, but looking good during a blowout and being the man at the helm of the offense are two very different propositions. The Texas defense should stay simple in practice, but show Brennan as much pre-snap complexity as possible. Texas needs cheap three and outs, Brennan miscues, and frustration. Letting Brennan get into a groove early with simple presnaps reads throwing to arguably the best pass catchers in the country is not a good idea. The former #4 rated pocket passer in the country has plenty of arm talent. Texas needs to assess his talent between the ears.

University of Texas El Paso

Dana Dimel (3rd year)
Offensive Background

2019 RECORD	3 YEAR TREND	5 YEAR TREND
1-11	**2-34**	**11-49**

RETURNING STARTERS	OFFENSE	DEFENSE
9	**4**	**5**

Last Meeting: 2016. Texas-41, UTEP- 7 Freshman quarterback Shane Buechele went 22 of 27 for 244 yards and 4 touchdowns while big Chris Warren thundered for 95 yards and a touchdown. UTEP star Aaron Jones rang up the Horns defense for 123 yards, including a 56-yard touchdown run, but he was the totality of a UTEP offense that passed for only 73 yards. Texas doubled up UTEP in total yardage 416-208 and cruised to a 34-point win in Austin. UTEP is 0-5 all-time against the Longhorns and has lost the last three games by an average score of 49-9. The real highlight of the series occurred in 2008 when ESPN cameras caught a young woman offering her boyfriend a helping hand while perched on a picturesque mountain looking down at the Sun Bowl. ESPN cameramen focused on the white glove treatment, much to the amusement of viewers. Texas won that game 42-13, but the action in the crowd was the real winner.

Overview

UTEP football has been terrible of late, winning only two of their last thirty-six games. This should be the worst team Texas has played in the Tom Herman era, though 2017 San Jose State would like to state its case if it can make it to the jury box without tripping. UTEP has always struggled to recruit and win in El Paso, but even when UTEP was a bad football team of the 4-8 or 5-7 variety, they featured desert gems like current New York Giant guard Will Hernandez or Green Bay running back Aaron Jones. We could grade individual Texas players in those match-ups and see how they fared. Those days are long gone. This is one of the worst rosters in FBS football and head coach Dana Dimel (former longtime Kansas State assistant, former head coach at Wyoming and Houston) has done little to improve it. His career 32-61 coaching record is well-earned, going 8-26 at a Houston Cougar job that has been exploited repeatedly as a platform for coaches to land bigger jobs at Baylor (Briles), Texas (Herman), Texas A&M (Sumlin), and even the Houston

Oilers (Jack Pardee). Dimel was fired in H-Town and somehow managed to wrangle another head coaching gig. Of interest to Texas fans is that 2019 UTEP starting quarterback Kai Locksley, a former Longhorn transfer, was arrested in early summer 2019 for a weapons charge, minor drug possession, DUI, and making a terroristic threat. Locksley was reinstated to the team in time for August practice and started for the Miners as they went 1-11. UTEP's primary terroristic threat was the prospect of their fans being forced to watch them play football.

Strengths: Delicious Mexican food

Running back Quardraiz Wadley did not exactly raze opposing defenses, but the big back (6'0, 220) has some power and shiftiness, rushing for a team high 627 yards and 7 touchdowns in 2018 before missing all of 2019 with a toe injury. Deion Hankins and Joshua Fields complement him in what should be a passable FBS backfield.

Defensive end Praise Amaewhule returns after leading the team in sacks last year with three. He projects as an all-conference level talent but the preview holds out hope that he will transfer to Oklahoma State and join Cowboy linebacker Amen Ogbongbemiga to form the Praise-Amen tackling duo. A defensive pairing worthy of reverence, if not worship.

Weaknesses: QB, OL, DL, LB, DB

The Miners were ranked 119th in the country in scoring offense. They lack talent, the offensive line is a sieve, and their defense managed only 12 sacks to go with a nationwide low 39 tackles for loss. Sophomore wide receiver Jacob Cowing flashed real ability as a deep threat, averaging 17.7 yards per catch in an offense that struggled to throw the ball. He is a legitimate pass catcher with near elite quickness that should warrant Longhorn attention. Dimel will try to upgrade Miner talent with an influx of JUCOs and transfers, but unlike the time-honored Kansas State model on which he was nurtured, these players are not that good, Dimel has done a poor job with program infrastructure, and some of them are not football focused. Using advanced metrics to explain UTEP football is a bit like using a Nobel prize winning physicist to explain a third grader's knowledge of quantum mechanics, but the Miners were ranked 129th out of 130 programs in FEI defense last year. Special teams checked in at dead last. Yep, 130th. Encouragingly, the UTEP offense ranked 122nd out of 130, so let's all agree that offense drives the engine of this football team.

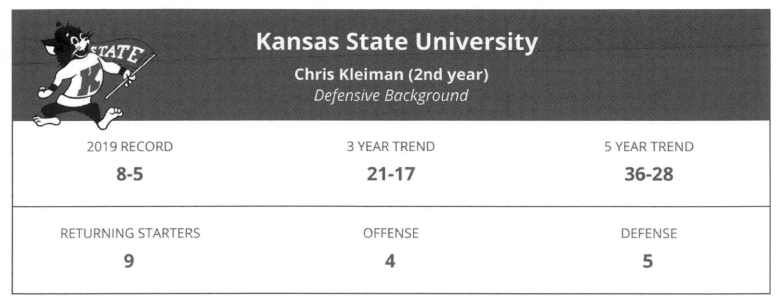

Kansas State University

Chris Kleiman (2nd year)
Defensive Background

2019 RECORD	3 YEAR TREND	5 YEAR TREND
8-5	**21-17**	**36-28**

RETURNING STARTERS	OFFENSE	DEFENSE
9	**4**	**5**

Last Meeting: Texas-27, Kansas State- 24. Cameron Dicker drilled a 26-yard game-winning field goal as time expired to seal the victory in Austin. Keaontay Ingram paced the Longhorn with a big rushing day, gaining 139 yards on 16 carries and scoring two touchdowns. Sam Ehlinger was an efficient 22 of 29 for 263 yards passing, exploiting both Duvernay and Johnson (each had 110 yards receiving) for easy completions against soft coverage. Texas went down 14-0 early in the 1st quarter as Todd Orlando's defense looked thoroughly unprepared for anything the Wildcats did. The Cats even stole an easy touchdown by lining up wide receiver Malik Knowles at running back. Knowles slipped out of the backfield unnoticed for any easy 70-yard touchdown catch. The Longhorns actually threatened to go down 21-0 if not for an outstanding individual effort from safety Brandon Jones, who forced a Kansas State fumble deep in Texas territory. That play turned the game as the defense found its composure, stopped blitzing randomly and exposing the secondary, and the Longhorn offense began to methodically run the ball and exploit soft Cat coverages on early downs. Kansas State's only other touchdown came on a 98-yard kickoff return. Texas narrowly edged a veteran Kansas State team who, in characteristic Wildcat fashion, made themselves a hard out.

Overview

Chris Klieman was tasked with continuing Bill Snyder's recent legacy of winning in the margins of the game and in his first season in Manhattan, he did just that, guiding a senior-laden Wildcat roster to a solid year and an exciting upset over Oklahoma, a win over Iowa State at home, a fun road win over Mississippi State, and a near victory over Texas in Austin. They controlled the clock, played great third down defense, limited possessions, did not turn it over, and owned pace. Masterful Snyder-esque stuff. They also lost to West Virginia in a game where they were made to play left-handed by the Mountaineer run defense, and took another loss when they failed to open the offense up sufficiently in a close bowl loss to Navy. Off the field, Klieman piloted the ship deftly through Kansas State factions still harboring some bitter feelings over succession and the question of how to best honor Bill Snyder without the old coach power-playing an appointment of his son to succeed him.

Now Klieman has a team that is more truly his and not just a tenured inheritance. To that point, Kansas State is fairly inexperienced, ranking 76th in the FBS in returning production, losing four offensive line starters and veteran defenders at every level of the defense. Historically, the Wildcats can control pace and clock with the best of them, but ultimately their ability to score enough points within that construct is their determinant of success. Whenever Kansas State put 24+ on the scoreboard, they were undefeated. When they did not? They went 1-5. That does not mean that Kansas State should install a fast break offense, but it does suggest that winning in the margins can become losing in the margins if a lack of experience erodes the program's subtle advantages. Kansas State finds itself in a great place on the Longhorn schedule: a home game in Manhattan right before Oklahoma. If you believe in trap games, Kansas State is digging a spiked pit and covering it up with leaves and branches as we speak. If Texas consents to playing Kansas State's game and starts the game sleepwalking as they did last year in Austin, they might just blunder into that cat hole. Particularly if the Wildcats can bait it with an Instagram like. The hope is that the new staff will provide the focus and game plan necessary to take care of business on the road against a team that might be able to dig pits, but should lose in the trenches.

Strengths: QB, DE, OLB, FB/TE, Special Teams

As in 2018, quarterback Skylar Thompson is quietly one of the better returning quarterbacks in the Big 12. In a league where quarterback statistics seem to come easy (and sometimes cheaply) in wide open offenses, Thompson is asked to manage the game, convert a lot of big downs, and win the game within the constraints of a very particular offensive approach. He still threw for 2315 yards last year at 7.8 yards per attempt. Impressive given the lack of talent and experience in the Wildcat receiving corps last year. Thompson is just dangerous enough as a runner, chipping in 405 yards rushing and 11 rushing touchdowns. He has 19 rushing touchdowns over his career. In the red zone, expect a Skylar Thompson quarterback draw, lead, or sweep. Bank on it. Thompson will have an inexperienced offensive line in front of him this year with JAG (just a guy) running backs. Given the young talent at wide receiver coming into its own and a solid pass catching tight end/fullback, the Wildcats may need to throw the ball around a bit more than they would like.

Elijah Sullivan and Wyatt Hubert are both high level, if contrasting, defenders. Sullivan is an undersized linebacker (210 pounds) who looks and runs like a safety but can bring the thunder when needed. He led Kansas State in tackles last year and will do so again. He also allows the Cats to run some pretty interesting coverage combinations and they certainly don't mind matching him on a running back or slot receiver when required. Hubert is a big, country strong defensive end with a good rip move and solid quickness off of the ball. Hubert was a deserved 1st Team All-Big 12 selection with 7 sacks and 12.5 tackles for loss; and a dominating force in Kansas State's win over Oklahoma. Outside of West Virginia's Darius Stills, you will be hard pressed to find a more potentially impactful defensive lineman on the Texas schedule.

Kansas State had the third best special teams unit in the country last year. They led the nation in kick return efficiency as Joshua Youngblood took back three kickoffs for touchdowns, including a 98 yarder against the Longhorns. That he did it as a true freshman is even more impressive. His outstanding 35.9 yards per kick return average was key to Kansas State winning the battle of hidden yards last year. Senior placekicker Blake Lynch - all 5-5, 150 pounds of him - also returns and he is 33 of 37 on field goals in his career. That 89.2% mark is the best in school history and ranks in the Top 5 of all active kickers in the country. Lynch was 19 of 21 last year and he is considered effectively automatic inside of 42 yards. The special teams unit was coordinated by Sean Snyder, son of Bill, now at USC. Snyder won multiple Special Teams Coach of the Year awards in his time in Manhattan and was arguably the top college special teams coach in the country. Whether the unit takes a step back without his leadership remains to be seen.

Weaknesses: OL, RB, DT

The Wildcats will build out their offensive line around premier interior run blocker guard Josh Rivas, who was excellent last year, but the rest of the unit is green. Certainly, by Kansas State's "every offensive line starter should be married with two kids and a mortgage" standards. Seasoned Wildcatologists know that transitional Kansas State offensive lines always do a fine job of coming together faster than expected, but from a physicality standpoint, second year two and three stars tend to have a rocky transition against high level defensive lines. With two redshirt freshmen offensive tackles slated to start in combination with only one upperclassman in the starting five, playing keepaway ball control gets a lot harder. Historically, good Texas defensive lines have been able to inflict sacks, tackles for loss, and negative plays on these lesser units. Assuming Texas does not assign edge support to a safety in Tarrytown, the Longhorn defense should present some real challenges for the Cats. It's hard to play ball control offense on 3rd and 9.

The Kansas State wide receivers are more dangerous than is commonly perceived. Joshua Youngblood and Malik Knowles are good young players getting better, but running back is unremarkable. Absent highly coordinated offensive line play and without a special runner of the Darren Sproles variety who can run the line's blocking better than it is, Kansas State's fundamental ball control proposition is on shaky ground. Runs that end with a one-yard gain instead of a quality back lurching forward for two more really matter in this offense. Fullback/tight end Nick Lenners is a handful as a blocker and play action pass catcher, but first team running back Harry Trotter is no wizard. His backup Tyler Burns is a big, strong athlete who could take over, but young Joe Ervin and Jacardia Wright are unknowns.

Kansas State lost defensive coordinator Scottie Hazelton to Michigan State and their new head coach Mel Tucker. You may remember Hazelton as the splendidly bearded individual on the Wildcat sideline who looked like General Longstreet crossed with a roadie for ZZ Top. Hazelton's generalship included a secret schematic sauce of 3rd down defense (a Big 12 league leading 28% 3rd down conversion defense) that was hugely responsible for the Cats winning eight games. On a per play basis, the Cats were unimpressive on defense. But third downs were magic and not the Harry Trotter kind. However, Scottie has been beamed away to an exotic world of cold winds and casseroles, replaced by Wildcat assistant Joe Klanderman. Klanderman may be a fine hire and he has a successful history with his head coach as an assistant, but he is totally unproven against Big 12 offenses. Klanderman has promised a more attacking defense, but the Cats lost their defensive line outside of Wyatt Hubert. That unit, excluding Hubert, was hardly game-altering, struggled to get pressure, and the replacements do not profile any better. So what exactly is Klanderman attacking *with*? A lot of Wyatt Hubert and positive self-talk. A likely erosion in 3rd down defense is another data point suggesting that Kansas State's careful alchemical formula may not be replicable without some essential 2019 components.

University of Oklahoma

Lincoln Riley (4th year)
Offensive Background

2019 RECORD	3 YEAR TREND	5 YEAR TREND
12-2	**36-6**	**58-10**

RETURNING STARTERS	OFFENSE	DEFENSE
16	**8**	**8**

Last Meeting: Oklahoma- 34, Texas- 27. The score was closer than the game felt as Texas scored its final touchdown with 1:49 left on the clock and trailed by double digits for much of the contest. The story of the game is that the Texas coaches lost it long before the opening kickoff in the Cotton Bowl. The Sooners defense registered a season high nine sacks and fifteen tackles for loss. Eight different Sooners registered a sack and Sam Ehlinger took multiple brutal hits while logging 23 carries. Offensively, the Sooners did about what they wanted, but were betrayed by two key Jalen Hurts first half turnovers (Hurts fumbled on the Texas 27-yard line after a long run and then threw an interception in the Longhorn end zone to Brandon Jones) that cost them certain points. CeeDee Lamb had 10 catches for 171 yards and 3 touchdowns. All other Sooner receivers totaled six catches for 64 yards. Oklahoma dominated running the ball, compiling 276 yards on only 38 carries, repeatedly exploiting tissue soft edge run support with numbers by virtue of simple alignment. Offensively, poised freshman Roschon Johnson inspired with a 57-yard run and 118 total yards from scrimmage.

Overview

Lincoln Riley is 36-6 entering his fourth year as the head coach in Norman, and has already posted three consecutive 12-2 seasons, earned three Big 12 titles, grabbed three college football playoff berths, boasts two Heisman trophy winning quarterbacks, and cemented his reputation as a quarterback whisperer by evolving a limited Jalen Hurts into a Heisman runner up drafted in the 2nd round. On the heels of Baker Mayfield and Kyler Murray being the 1st picks of their respective draft classes. That is the factual and perceptual headwind that Texas faces when recruiting against Oklahoma for any offensive prospect. If Texas does not like it, they should get started changing it. The most consistent program in the Big 12 is looking to do it all over again with a brand-new quarterback, a talented if unproven wide receiver corps, a stable offensive line, and improved depth on defense.

Last year, the Sooners averaged 42 points and 548 yards per game and blew through twelve of fourteen opponents like a gale through a paper airplane factory. Or a Sooner named Gale blowing through the discount bin at the Marlboro outlet. Whichever gale you prefer, the only Big 12 opponent that defended the Sooners adequately was Baylor and, of course, a red-hot LSU pieced them up in the playoffs. On the other side of the ball, the Sooner defense improved substantially from 2018 (their 104th FEI ranking improved 35 spots to 69th in 2019) by swapping out the failing Mike Stoops for Alex Grinch, but were still vulnerable to great game plans with veteran offensive lines (Kansas State, Iowa State) and racked up pass interference calls like flatlands credit card debt. Despite calling off the dogs early, LSU had 693 yards of offense in their 63-point playoff barrage, exposing Oklahoma's press coverage and lack of pass rush, but it is sad consolation for Longhorn fans to live vicariously through another team punishing their conference bully.

The Sooners rank 103rd in college football in returning offensive production. That is troubling data on its face for Sooner fans, but it obscures causal reality if misinterpreted: the Sooner offense is a river and Riley is its source. He will turn the spigot and the waters will flow again. Texas needs to make the Red River run crimson with some smashed mouths if they want to change the Lincoln Riley, boy genius, narrative. Until proven otherwise, the Sooners are the default choice for a Big 12 title.

Strengths: QB, WR, RB, OL, Lincoln Riley

All you need to know about the respect level for Lincoln Riley's offensive system is that redshirt freshman Spencer Rattler, who has attempted all of 11 college passes, and has not even been officially announced as the Sooner starter, debuted in 4th place in the preseason Heisman odds. That is not preseason media hype, but actionable Vegas action. Rattler was the consensus #1 quarterback recruit in the 2019 class despite missing his senior season for a violation of team rules. The 6-0, 200-pound signal caller is known for having a pure arm and good feel for the passing game. Rattler is mobile enough but only a decent runner. That aspect of the Oklahoma offense that featured Hurts and Murray will be shelved for more of a Baker Mayfield distributor approach. Rattler will run opportunistically, but not very often by design. Rattler is known for a release as quick as his namesake and he has more than an abundance of confidence, crossing the border into obnoxiousness. In short, he is the perfect Sooner quarterback nemesis for Texas. Chris Ash needs to find some king snakes and mongooses.

One would think that losing Texas tormenter CeeDee Lamb would cripple the Sooner receiving corps, but the remaining talent there is good and the system will highlight their abilities. Charleston Rambo caught 43 balls last year for 743 yards last year and blue-chip talents like Theo Wease, Trejan Bridges, and Jadon Haselwood are just waiting to grab their share of the offense. Longhorns fans hoping for a dropoff in the Sooner passing game will likely be disappointed. Rather than the CeeDee Lamb show, the Sooner passing game will be repurposed to a distributed load with a much better pure passer pulling the trigger.

The Sooner offensive line returns four starters, including All-American center Creed Humphrey. Humphrey was terrific as a redshirt freshman in 2018, but his game actually took a step back in 2019, particularly in pass protection. Texas needs to show Keondre Coburn the film of what his twin body type, Baylor's Brayvion Roy, did to Humphrey in their match-up. Roy had five pressures and repeatedly got under Humphrey's pads, pushing the big center back into Jalen Hurts. Styles make fights and Coburn could be his Rocky Balboa. Guard Marquis Hayes is very good - a down-and-dirty 6-5, 330-pound masher - who complements his guard counterpart Tyrese Robinson, who goes 6-3, 330 and can also move the pile in the running game. Tackle is less impressive, as adequate Adrian Ealy will hold down the right side after starting 12 games last year. Erik Swenson (benched for part of 2019) and Stacey Wilkins (blue chip redshirt freshman) will battle for the left tackle spot. The interior offensive line is the fundamental strength of this unit and they are led by Bill Bedenbaugh, who is probably one of the best two or three college offensive line coaches in the country.

Oklahoma running back Tre Sermon transferred to the Ohio State Buckeyes. It is a sign of their talent and depth at the position that they will shrug that off with big play runner Kennedy Brooks, who averaged 6.5 yards per carry while compiling 1011 yards, and former JUCO transfer Rhamondre Stevenson, who chipped in 515 yards at an amazing 8 yards per tote. Stevenson is a big back who evokes comparisons to LeGarrette Blount. Given the Sooner offensive line composition and run blocking acumen between the tackles, expect to see him split the backfield snaps with the speedy Brooks. TJ Pledger waits in the wings should something happen to either. The Sooners have good running backs running behind even better schemes.

Weaknesses- DL, DB

Star strongside defensive end and five technique Ronnie Perkins is appealing a five game NCAA drug suspension. If he misses the Texas game that would be a major blow to the Sooner pass rush and their run-stopping ability, further exposing an otherwise merely adequate defensive line. Marcus Stripling is a very good backup for Perkins that Grinch will try to get into the line-up full time when Perkins returns, but the interior has a gaping hole left by departed nose tackle Neville Gallimore. His raw power and ability to collapse pockets will be missed by the Sooners defensive line and Alex Grinch's interior stunt concepts. Gallimore was the bruising power forward setting bone rattling picks that set up the departed Kenneth Murray's lay-up runs (17 tackles for loss) to the backfield. They are counting on JUCO Perrion Winfrey to provide what Gallimore did and that is improbable at best. Oklahoma's front looks great on the hoof and can be a handful executing Grinch's stunts in concert with the Sooner linebackers, but offensive lines that kept their heads aided by solid game planning whipped them in some key contests. And that was with the departed Gallimore wrecking shop inside. Kansas State's senior laden offensive line worked the Sooners over pretty well despite the Wildcat offense not hitting a play longer than 26 yards in a 48-41 home victory that featured six Kansas State rushing touchdowns. Iowa State's experienced offensive line and a good game plan turned off the Sooner stunt game like a cheap lamp. Against the Cyclones, the Sooners had 0 sacks and 3 tackles for loss while surrendering 41 points. If Texas will demonstrate a little poise and some decent game planning, particularly sans Ronnie Perkins, this bunch looks a lot scarier than they play.

The Sooners return four defensive backs, but lose 1st team All Big 12 cornerback Parnell Motley. While "weakness" may be a stretch in describing the Sooner defensive backs, characterizing them as a team strength is a stretch the other way. Let us call them what they are: a possible opportunity. The smallish Sooners intercepted only 3 balls over their last 11 games last year and led the Big 12 conference in pass interference calls. The latter is as much a feature as a bug of their defensive philosophy, but failing to turn opponents over and giving up a new set of downs with a penalty puts a great deal of pressure on Oklahoma's defense. Senior cornerback Tre Brown can run, but he is shaky when the ball is in the air. On the other side, sophomore Jaden Davis will compete with Tre Norwood, returning from a blown-out knee. At

nickel safety, Brendan Radley-Hiles is best described as a talented knucklehead, evidenced by his ejection from the playoff game, unsportsmanlike flags, and a tendency to dive for shoelaces after incessant chatter about who he is going to light up. He is That Guy and Oklahoma always seems to have a few. Delarrin Turner-Yell is their most consistent safety in most facets and should return 100% from the broken collarbone he sustained in December. Pat Fields is coming into his own, but none of the Sooner defensive backs leap off of the screen. They are not very big - collectively they run under 5-11 and around 190 pounds. Texas needs to make a point of hunting match-ups that put the Sooners in run support, and force them to tackle stronger Texas receivers in space. Oklahoma needs to get bullied and that is as much gameplan as mindset.

Grinch's schemes, deprived of strong cornerback play or instinctive safeties tackling well and ranging over the top, effectively offer an offensive Pass/Fail test. If you have the athletes and execution, things can get ugly for Oklahoma real fast. The Sooners were good on 3rd down (31.6% opponent conversion rate) but were terrible at turning offenses over with 11 turnovers forced in 14 games, ranking 121st in the country. While turnovers can be partially attributed to the simple randomness of how the ball bounces, some portion of blame must be affixed to a secondary that proved incapable of making plays on the ball.

West Virginia University
Neal Brown (2nd year)
Offensive Background

2019 RECORD	3 YEAR TREND	5 YEAR TREND
5-7	**20-17**	**38-25**

RETURNING STARTERS	OFFENSE	DEFENSE
16	**8**	**8**

Last Meeting: Texas- 42, Texas- 31 The Longhorns secured a road victory in a tough environment against a physically outmatched but feisty West Virginia. For the game, Texas totaled 427 total yards (211 passing, 216 rushing) but it took 82 plays at 5.2 yards per snap to get there. It was an unnecessary grind that included a tough to watch 3rd quarter in which Texas had 5 possessions (created by Mountaineer turnovers) that totaled 49 yards on 22 plays. Ehlinger's first half stat line was a healthy 13 of 21 for 176 yards and 2 touchdowns. Second half stat line? 5 of 12 for 35 yards and 1 interception. Roschon Johnson was a bright spot totaling 121 yards on 21 carries and averaged 5.8 yards a pop. The Texas defense forced four turnovers and repeatedly set up the offense with short fields in the second half. That was absolutely decisive to the game outcome as the Longhorns scored 21 points off of turnovers to West Virginia's 3. Two of those interceptions were incredibly athletic plays (a phenomenal Jamison one-handed deep ball pick, and an opportunistic B.J. Foster tip drill). Two were very solid plays on terrible throws (Jamison's break on a poor Kendall outside route, Adeoye's drop into a poor Kendall read). Still, West Virginia showed some grit in Morgantown. Let's see what they bring to Austin.

Overview

You have to respect Neal Brown's first year at West Virginia. The former head coach at Troy (31-8 over his last three seasons) took over a talent depleted program and did a nice job of winning over the remaining players while pursuing his guys on the recruiting trail. How talent depleted were the Mountaineers? Dana Holgorsen saw what his 2019 depth chart looked like, reflected on his inability to find a good whiskey bar open at 1:30am on a Tuesday night in Morgantown, checked out of the Ramada Inn suite that he was living in, and hightailed it to the Houston Cougars, leaving the Mountaineer program to the mercy of the transfer portal. The exodus was biblical and Brown did the best he could with a thinly talented roster. While the prospectus correctly predicted West Virginia's descent from a 8-4 record in 2018 to a 5-7 team in 2019, the Mountaineers showed some heart down the backstretch of the season, taking down Kansas State and TCU on the road to close out the year. They had nothing to play for but got after it nonetheless. A sign of pluck that speaks well of the internal culture that Brown is developing. Brown's 2020 recruiting class also reflects well of his longer-term plans. West Virginia is a tough place to recruit to and for years they have inordinately relied on a contrarian recruiting model: courting JUCOs, grad transfers, and disgruntled players from name programs that grew weary of a lack of playing time or found themselves on the wrong side of the law. Brown is making a concerted effort to grow his talent within the program and not rely on mercenaries for hire.

His 2020 class ranked 4th in the Big 12 and #37 nationally - not a number that will turn heads - but if you dig a bit deeper into the class you will find an assortment of athletes that are exactly who they should be targeting. Brown is identifying developmental football players who can run and finding big frames that can be filled out in the weight room. West Virginia has always been able to find skill players, but this class featured quality on both lines. West Virginia has little business out-recruiting Oklahoma State or Baylor from a location or resource standpoint, but that is precisely what they did. They are also off to a good start in 2021.

Unfortunately for Neal Brown, the inland mountains and hollows are not immune from the current societal tides. Defensive coordinator Vic Koenning, who crafted some really fine late season gameplans with short-handed personnel, coaxing the Mountaineer defense into playing above its talent level in most contests, was placed on administrative leave after allegations of player mistreatment, racial insensitivity, and generally being a jerk. Whether those accusations have a substantive basis will determine the coordinator's fate. Not a great time to potentially lose your best coordinator. In addition, West Virginia will field a baseline talent level that is still clearly in the bottom half of the Big 12. Their offense, despite some bright spots at wide receiver, also looks like a long-term project. While some prognosticators are touting West Virginia for a bowl and a winning Big 12 record, that seems unlikely. West Virginia is on a positive long-term trajectory, but may still level out, or even take a step back, in 2020.

Strengths: WR, DL

The West Virginia wide receiver corps was a very respectable unit despite having arguably some of the worst quarterback play in the Big 12 last year. Redshirt sophomore Sam James is an elusive wideout with good hands. He grabbed 69 balls last year for 677 yards. That pedestrian yards per catch average is not reflective of his speed, but rather a West Virginia offense that relied on getting the ball out quickly. T.J. Simmons is back after a 35 catch, 455-yard effort and the big inside receiver (6-2, 205) is a reliable pass catcher who transferred in from Alabama three years ago. Little Winston Wright saw minimal action as a true freshman, but the waterbug is a mismatch in tight quarters and should see increased snaps. Finally, Bryce Wheaton projects as the big-bodied physical mismatch (6-3, 220) that West Virginia needs. He averaged 16.8 yards per catch on only 12 catches, but he should see extensive action in 2020. This is not a world-beating group, but certainly a relative strength for a team that needs playmakers.

If you want to see good defensive line play, go find #55 and #56 on the West Virginia defense. The Stills brothers could be as sporadic in their play as the quality of the backwoods moonshine conceived in their namesake, but when they brought it, their play had a kick that left quarterbacks wobbling. Darius and Dante Stills are two of the most disruptive defensive players in the league. Dante was a 1st Team All Big 12 performer, totaling 14.5 tackles for loss and 8 sacks. Brother Darius, 2nd Team All Big 12, had 6 sacks and 12 tackles for loss of his own. Dante is a powerfully built 6-1, 290-pound three-man front defensive end who uses his low base and quickness to wreak havoc on slower, taller offensive lineman and pinball into the backfield. Darius is not as bursty as his brother, but the 6-3, 280-pounder is just as strong and has better length. Darius really thrives when Dante demands double team attention. He was dominant in the Mountaineer upset of North Carolina State with two sacks and multiple pressures. West Virginia lacks depth here (Stills waters do not run deep) but the front-line quality is high.

Weaknesses: QB, OL, RB

Former Bowling Green starting quarterback Jarrett Doege (39 touchdowns and 15 interceptions in two years as a starter there) expects to be the starter, but former Sooner Austin Kendall is still lurking after a turnover marred 2019 where he threw 12 touchdowns and 10 interceptions before going out with a late season chest injury. Kendall consistently practices better than Doege, but game play has been another matter. Doege did not necessarily shine in relief last year (120 attempts, 79 completions, 818 yards, 7 touchdowns, 3 interceptions, 6.8 yards per attempt), but he did not turn it over carelessly, made a few clutch throws, and allowed West Virginia's defense to carry the day in late season wins over TCU and Kansas State. That consistency may speak to Neal Brown as he seeks to raise the level of a moribund offense. If Doege can raise his game to consistently solid, West Virginia may have a path forward to a possible minor bowl game, but the upside at quarterback is just not there to consider this unit anything but a limiting factor in their season.

The West Virginia offensive line struggled mightily to open holes for their running backs and the loss of tackles Colton McKivitz to the NFL Draft and Kolby Wickline to graduation does not help matters. Returning starting running back Leddie Brown, surprisingly not the name of a Puritan midwife, averaged 3.4 yards per carry while leading the Mountaineers with a scant 367 rushing yards. The Mountaineers collectively averaged a putrid 2.6 yards per carry overall. That is reflective of a talent deficit at running back and on the offensive line, but gone too are Dana Holgorsen's spread running schemes that alway seemed to manufacture good situations for his runners. Neal Brown's Mountaineers have shown no comparable coaching facility. While there is no way but up for a ground game that averaged only 73.4 yards per game, the mechanisms for a significant improvement are not apparent. In combination with a passing game that struggled to get the ball down the field, it is little wonder that West Virginia was ranked as the 101st best offense in the FBS by advanced statistical measures. If there is a bright spot, they were solid in pass protection, surrendering only 21 sacks, but their loss of the two aforementioned tackles will compromise that carryover to 2020 despite an intact interior offensive line. The replacements outside are unknowns, with a fairly poor recruiting pedigree. Any way you slice it, things do not look good for the Blue and Gold up front or for their offense in general. They will be a grinding unit that will need to feature the short passing game.

Texas Tech University

Matt Wells (2nd year)
Offensive Background

2019 RECORD	3 YEAR TREND	5 YEAR TREND
4-8	**15-22**	**27-35**

RETURNING STARTERS	OFFENSE	DEFENSE
14	**6**	**8**

Last Meeting: Texas-49 , Texas Tech-24 The Longhorns eventually teed off on Tech at home, crushing an inferior team in a tailspin. The game was far too competitive in the first few moments as Tech's offense moved the ball easily and opened up an early 14-0 lead. The Horns responded with a furious 22-point second quarter to take a 28-21 halftime lead and then asserted themselves from then on for an enjoyable home win. Sam Ehlinger was a nearly flawless 19 of 27 for 348 yards while also running for an easy 83 yards. He also hit a second quarter 75-yard touchdown strike to Devin Duvernay to tie the game at 21 and turn the tide of whatever momentum Tech had built. Duvernay totaled 199 yards on only 6 catches to cap a brilliant regular season. Jake Smith broke his freshman slump with 3 catches for 51 yards and a touchdown, and steady Roschon Johnson powered the ground assault with 105 yards rushing and three touchdowns. Texas Tech had their moments on offense. Erik Ezukanma caught 7 balls for 135 yards and a touchdown while backup KeSean Carter had a career high 150 yards on 11 catches. Prior to that game, the reserve had 16 catches for 153 yards for the season. SaRodorick Thompson added 86 yards rushing, exhibiting some nice burst. Longhorn safeties Brandon Jones and Chris Brown combined for an amazing 20 solo tackles to pace the defense and were crucial in stabilizing the Horns defense after a poor start.

Overview

Last year, the preview projected Texas Tech as a potentially interesting conference spoiler and general pest if they could meet two conditions. First, Tech quarterback Alan Bowman must remain healthy. Second, they must find something resembling a defense so that they could hold the leads that Bowman might grant them. Denied and denied. Bowman was lost for the season to a shoulder injury after starting only three games and the Red Raider defense couldn't get push on a toddler on a swing. The team went 4-8 with a legitimate late season collapse that included a loss to Kansas. But they also lost four games by a field goal or less. Texas Tech is not really that terrible. They just play that way. Anyone handicapping the 2019 Big 12 rookie coaching hires for future program success currently have Neal Brown and Chris Klieman outpacing Matt Wells and Les Miles, but we will see what 2020 brings. The Red Raiders have a roster capable of playing solid football if they can get some defensive guidance and a healthy quarterback. Offensively, Tech moved the ball, but ranked 51st in FEI, demonstrating that they thrived on empty calories between the 20's. The proposition from 2019 remains largely unchanged: keep Alan Bowman on his feet and play passable defense. The Red Raider schedule is forgiving, with a strength of schedule ranked 52nd in the nation. Their non-conference slate should instill confidence: UTEP, Alabama State, Arizona. UTEP's woes are detailed elsewhere in this preview, Alabama State is known primarily for its band and dancers, and Arizona is coached by Kevin Sumlin. A 3-0 start would do wonders for surety and player buy-in. Road trips to Ames and Stillwater offer no favors, but they get West Virginia, Baylor, Texas, and Kansas all at home. No excuse not to win three of those conference home games. The potential for climbing out of the conference basement to respectability is there, but bad luck and some bad coaching decisions have thwarted a once respectable program. Mike Leach went 84-43 in Lubbock and never had a losing season over ten years. In the ten years since, they are 61-65 with six losing seasons. Maybe next time, keep Adam James in that closet.

Strengths- QB(?), WR, Interior OL

A healthy Alan Bowman is a good pocket passing quarterback. When healthy, he consistently demonstrates accuracy and the ability to fit the ball through tight windows. Sometimes that urge to thread the needle burns him with interceptions, but every West Texas cowboy knows that it's easier to pull back on the reins than to constantly have to dig in the spurs. An injured Alan Bowman ensures the near certainty of a losing season, unless backup Maverick Mcivor weaves some Maverick magic of his own. The redshirt freshman and former San Angelo high school star (and son of Longhorn QB Rick Mcivor) does not lack attributes, but suffered a broken leg in practice before the 2019 season which robbed him of a year of development. Without Bowman, Tech is 2-10 over the last two years. Bowman, now a redshirt sophomore, has battled through a collapsed lung and broken shoulder to return to action, but the Red Raiders have to protect him better and Bowman has to protect himself by getting the ball out on time. Offensive coordinator David Yost (the former kindergarten teacher is still worth the Google image search, please do yourself the favor) can help his cause by beefing up his protections and picking his spots for the kill shots.

The Texas Tech pass catchers are talented and diverse, but volatile quarterback Jett Duffey was an unreliable distributor of the football. Alan Bowman has the potential to level them all up and even make a couple of them stars. Speedy and powerful sophomore Erik Ezukanma (6-2, 210) caught 42 balls for 664 yards and 4 touchdowns, small forward sized (6'6") red zone threat TJ Vasher grabbed 42 balls for 515 yards and 6 touchdowns, while shifty former walk-on Dalton Rigdon nabbed 34 receptions for 5 touchdowns. Ezukanma projects as the best all-around receiver, but Vasher is an experienced senior with 1756 career receiving yards and 19 touchdowns. Rigdon is another in the long history of underrecruited Tech receivers who manages to come up with that key catch. You know what is being implied. Here is another hint: *coach on the field.* Depth is very solid with former Nevada Wolfpack star McLane Mannix (26-248-3) and KeSean Carter (27-303-2) rounding out the rotation. This is a fine unit that underperformed due to Duffey's erratic play. They are simply waiting for the right distributor to exploit their skills.

Junior guard Jack Anderson was one of the most highly touted recruits to ever come to Lubbock and he has not disappointed in his Red Raider career. Last year was cut short by injury, ending 26 consecutive starts, but Anderson is back and should contend for 1st Team All Big 12 honors. Center Dawson Deaton gets no hype in Lubbock, but he had a good sophomore season. He is back to head up one of the better interior offensive line trios in the Big 12. Despite his 6-6 frame he does a good job with pad level. Redshirt sophomore Weston Wright plays right guard and the 6-6, 310 pounder is one of the better interior pass blockers you will find. One of the most striking things in reviewing Texas Tech's season was how well the interior offensive line played in pass protection. The offensive tackle spots are less certain, where they are breaking in new starters Casey Verhulst

and Wofford graduate transfer Josh Burger. If those two surprise, Tech could have a very good offensive line. If not, Bowman will need to get the ball out pretty quickly.

Weaknesses- DL, DB

Last year, the preview opined that Big 12 offenses would offer new defensive coordinator Keith Patterson a rude introduction to Big 12 play. Well, that happened. That was not just a comment on Patterson's available talent, but also an analysis of pressure philosophies that can too often come at the expense of soundness. Patterson spent much of the second half of the season getting dog cussed on the sideline by his head coach on television, which was not a great look for Texas Tech, but when your defense surrenders 9.2 yards per passing attempt and finishes 89th in national FEI rankings, sweet nothings are not going to be whispered into your headset. On the positive side, Patterson's defense did prove adept at forcing turnovers, keeping Tech in several games where they were otherwise gashed. Tech lost the best linebacker in the conference in the outstanding Jordyn Brooks (20 tackles for loss, 1st round draft pick by Seattle) and a powerful run-stopping defensive tackle in Broderick Washington. While eight starters return and they get back 80% of their top tacklers, until Patterson fully unscrews himself schematically, Texas Tech will not leave the bottom third of conference defenses.

Every year, Texas Tech enthusiasts offer defensive end Eli Howard as a breakout star because of his size (6-4, 275) and relentless West Texas motor. Every year, for three years running, Howard totals between 2.5 to 5.0

sacks with around 20 tackles on the season. In 30 career starts, Howard has 82 tackles and 12 career sacks. Ho-hum. More disconcertingly, his player picture on Red Raider Sports features a messy man bun that he spent way too much time on. Man buns degrade game impact. In his senior year, look for Eli Howard to break out. To a barber. The rest of the Texas Tech defensive line is unproven or thoroughly average. Linebacker Riko Jeffers is a fine player and will be their leading tackler.

Standout freshman cornerback Adrian Frye excelled in 2018 with 5 interceptions and All Big 12 honors, but defensive coordinator Keith Patterson puzzlingly moved him to safety, where he struggled to make an impact.

Frye moves back to cornerback in 2020, where he should have stayed to begin with. Stop making football hard for yourself, Patterson. Texas Tech had the worst pass defense in the Big 12 last year, but certainly not the worst personnel. They also lost safety Douglas Coleman, whose 8 interceptions led the Big 12. Coleman might be replaced by LSU graduate transfer Eric Monroe, who is heading to Lubbock via grad transfer. Monroe could not crack the first team in Baton Rouge, but may find West Texas talent levels more agreeable. Perhaps the proper personnel recalibration and better coaching will fix things back here, but until we see it, this is a team weakness with a lot to prove.

Baylor University

Dave Aranda (1st year)
Defensive Background

2019 RECORD	3 YEAR TREND	5 YEAR TREND
11-3	**19-20**	**36-29**

RETURNING STARTERS	OFFENSE	DEFENSE
9	**7**	**2**

Last Meeting Baylor- 24, Texas-10 Baylor dominated Texas defensively, forcing punts on the Longhorns first five possessions. The Longhorns finished the game 4 of 15 on 3rd down and Baylor racked up five sacks. Keaontay Ingram was a bright spot with a nice 68-yard run at the end of the first half but that encapsulated the totality of any meaningful Texas offense (that run before the half ended in a field goal). The Texas defense played well in the first half, but Baylor's offense made halftime adjustments and Texas did not respond. The Bears scored on their first three possessions of the second half, racking up 207 yards on only 26 plays. Denzel Mims had a big day with 7 catches for 125 yards and a touchdown. Staked to a 24-3 lead, Charlie Brewer exited the game at the 11-minute mark after sustaining a concussion and Baylor effectively ran clock for the remainder of the game. It was a disappointing performance, revealing a gap in maximization between two coaches who had both been hired at the same time three years prior.

Overview

Matt Rhule's terrific three-year turnaround at Baylor (1-11, 7-6, 11-3) earned him a NFL head coaching job and with his departure goes the continuity of a program rebuilt on Rhule's, well, rules. The defense he used to power Baylor's level up has largely scattered to the winds. Will Baylor's wins scatter with it? Rhule transformed a disastrous Baylor program with doggedly stubborn coaching and development. And he did it relatively quickly considering the state of the nationally detested pariah program that he took over. With a winning college quarterback in Charlie Brewer, deep threat Denzel Mims, and a rugged defense that squeezed every bit of ability out of its talent level, Baylor ended up with an 11-3 2019 squad that came very close to upsetting Oklahoma in Waco, then nearly stole the Big 12 title in Dallas in the rematch with their 3rd string quarterback leading a late rally.

LSU defensive coordinator Dave Aranda is a fine hire, but Aranda is stepping into a rebuild. Not the total overhaul of the Art Briles dumpster fire that Matt Rhule inherited, but a major talent reload, with a need to replace most of the key playing and coaching engines that drove Baylor's turnaround. Aranda tackles that challenge without the ability to hold spring practice or install his new system. For a first-year head coach leading a new staff, with only nine total returning starters, that has potential consequences. They open with Ole Miss in Houston, a team with similar circumstances starting over under new head coach Lane Kiffin. Yes, Kiffin is at Ole Miss now. Letting Lane Kiffin coach Ole Miss is like letting Tiger Woods manage a Perkins. And only Baylor would schedule Ole Miss at a neutral site on a Sunday, completely negating the primary benefit of playing the Rebels: pregame partying at the Grove and chatting up Southern belles looking for a ticket out of Pascagoula. Fortunately, Baylor gets Kansas, Incarnate Word, and Louisiana Tech before tackling Oklahoma in Norman. There will be some time to get their legs, but not enough. The Bears rank 108th in overall returning production and 127th in returning defensive production. The Bears also finished 2019 +11 in turnover margin, won five games by only one score or less, and their star quarterback sustained multiple concussions over the last few games of the 2019 season. That screams significant program regression. The 2020 Baylor Bears are not challenging for a Big 12 title. They are fighting for a winning season.

Strengths: QB(?), OT, Team speed

Charlie Brewer (son of former Longhorn QB Robert) played a significant role in elevating the Baylor program from his 1-11 freshman season debut to last year's playoff contender. Over three seasons, Brewer has thrown for 7742 yards and 51 touchdowns with only 20 interceptions in addition to 18 career rushing touchdowns. Brewer's game is about mobility, accuracy, touch and intelligence and his leadership and game experience are sorely needed to power an offense that will need to compensate for a diminished defense. That all comes with a caveat: Brewer's health. Sadly, Brewer has sustained at least three concussions in the last nine months. His senior season could be abbreviated, if not lost entirely. That elephant in the room is a mean, unsentimental mammoth. Gerry Bohanon is a capable runner, but questionable passer, while smooth Jacob Zeno throws a sharp, catchable ball. Zeno showed poise when called to face the Sooners in Arlington, completing a pair of deep passes (81 and 78 yards) against the Sooner secondary to bring the game to overtime. If Aranda wants the passing game to flourish with a speedy Baylor receiving corps, he had better give Zeno some first team reps in August.

About that receiving corps. Denzel Mims was the only truly game-altering athlete on the 2019 Baylor offense. The perimeter deep threat kept defenses honest and his 66 catch, 1020-yard, 12 touchdown production will be badly missed. Baylor will particularly miss all of the double teams he drew. Elusive and speedy Tyquan Thornton will be asked to match that output and he has legitimate big play potential, notching 45 balls for a 17.7 average last year. Thornton is tall and he can run, but his skinny frame is 25 pounds lighter than Mims and he must prove that he won't be muscled by press coverage as the #1 outside receiver. Baylor has legitimate speed at all of their skill positions, but no single receiver will bring what Mims did last year.

Connor Galvin has improved dramatically from his freshman year and the 6-7 athlete has grown his 250-pound frame into a 300-pound pass protector. Blake Bedier will join him at the other tackle spot and the JUCO transfer from Snow Junior College will build on last year's 12 starts to help Galvin address an offensive line that surrendered 38 sacks and far too many hits on Brewer last season. Bedier did not play high school football. Needless to say, his learning curve is still active, but the potential upside is promising. Both tackles will be better than last year and both will need to be if Baylor's offense has any chance of succeeding against quality defenses.

Weaknesses: DL, DB

The best defensive line in the Big 12 is gone. That is Big 12 Defensive Player of the Year James Lynch, All Big 12 nose tackle Brayvion Roy, and solid veteran James Lockhart. They formed the beating heart of the Baylor defense. Together, those three players compiled 25 sacks and 41 tackles for loss last year. No front in the conference could compare to that level of production and the players replacing them will struggle to match even half of that output from Aranda's preferred tite front (3 defensive linemen inside the offensive tackles).

JACK linebacker William Bradley-King is a promising graduate transfer, but Baylor's pass rush and run disruption is about to take a major hit. That will have a trickle-down effect to the Bear linebacking corps where Terrel Bernard will be cast in a more traditional inside linebacker role than the space and stunt player he was last year. The 2nd team All Big 12 performer is a welcome returnee for the depleted Bear defense, but it will be interesting to see how he adapts to a new defense and more blocking attention.

The Baylor defense returns experienced cornerbacks in Raleigh Texada and Kalon Barnes, but without Baylor's pass rush and excellent safety play from last season, how will those cornerbacks fare in a system that will dramatically expand their roles and responsibilities? Less help, heavier coverage burdens, and a longer clock for the quarterback are not classic enablers of cornerback play. At safety and their linebacker/safety hybrid, Baylor lost vast experience and playmaking. Departed free safety Grayland Arnold led the Bears with six interceptions and covered up a lot of warts for the Bears in the passing game. Henry Black was Baylor's most experienced enforcer (he played in 52 games in Waco) and he was a tough run stopper and strong tackler. Blake Lynch was the linebacker/safety hybrid who did it all and filled in where needed in coverage or at the line of scrimmage. Third safety Chris Miller was solid across the board, and like all of his cohorts, had dozens of games of starting experience under his belt. Replacements like Christian Morgan and J.T. Woods have their work cut out for them. If James Lynch and his defensive line cohorts were the heart of the Baylor defense, Baylor's losses in the middle back 7 were the lungs and brains. Helpful organs to have against spread offenses.

University of Kansas

Les Miles (2nd year at KU)
Offensive Background

2019 RECORD	3 YEAR TREND	5 YEAR TREND
3-9	**7-29**	**9-51**

RETURNING STARTERS	OFFENSE	DEFENSE
8	**5**	**3**

Last Meeting: Texas- 50, Kansas- 48. Down six starters to injuries and off-field suspensions, the Texas defense struggled with every fundamental aspect of football while allowing 569 yards and 48 points (KU was held under 50 by virtue of two blocked kicks and a missed field goal). Texas surrendered a seasonal high-water mark of offense to an eventual 3-9 Jayhawk team that scored a total of 31 points against Indiana State (24) and Coastal Carolina (7) in weeks prior. Orlando's safety blitzes, which vacated the middle of the field, were exploited by newly appointed Kansas offensive coordinator Brent Dearmon, who installed a RPO heavy gameplan during the Kansas bye week that targeted this exact tendency. Kansas converted 12 of 21 on money downs (57.1%) , including 2 for 2 on 4th down. They also easily converted a 2-point play to take the lead with 1:11 left in the game. Running back Pooka Williams sliced up Texas for 190 yards and Kansas quarterback Carter Stanley threw for 310. Fortunately, the Texas offense showed up, dropping 638 yards on the Jayhawks. Ehlinger was 31 of 44 for 399 yards and four

touchdowns while Keaontay Ingram provided 101 yards to go with Sam's 91 yards rushing. Ehlinger's 490 total yard effort was one of the biggest performances in Longhorn history. The game ultimately turned on special teams as Texas blocked multiple Kansas kicks (Roach, Ossai), D'Shawn Jamison returned one of them, and Cameron Dicker nailed the game winner as time expired. Texas narrowly averted a humiliating home loss to a 21.5-point road underdog.

Overview

Last year, the preview nailed a 3-9 prediction for the Jayhawks, but accurately predicting degrees of failure is not that enviable a skill. Kansas is a program still trying to stagger out of disarray and ruin, led by a colorful head coach padding out his retirement accounts. The Jayhawks had flashes of competitiveness last season: upsetting Boston College on the road, edging Texas Tech for their only Big 12 win, narrowly losing to West Virginia, and succumbing on a last second field goal to Texas (gulp) on the road. Beyond those victories - moral and actual - Kansas was pretty bad, dropping a game to Coastal Carolina, getting blown out by TCU, Oklahoma, Kansas State, Oklahoma State, and Baylor. When Kansas was competitive in a game last year, it was usually a result of their opponent royally screwing up or innovative midseason promoted offensive coordinator Brent Dearmon installing a nice little game plan. Dearmon received a battlefield promotion from offensive analyst to offensive coordinator on October 6th during the Jayhawk bye week and then tormented Todd Orlando in Austin just a few days later. If Kansas shocks the Big 12 and the country with a competitive season, look to Dearmon and the Kansas skill triumvirate of Pooka, Parchment, and Robinson as the primary cause. Les Miles will be off somewhere saying silly things and chewing on foliage, which won't stop sportswriters from proclaiming his wily coaching intangibles as the root cause of Jayhawk progress.

Strengths: RB, WR

Next to Chuba Hubbard, Pooka Williams remains the most exciting runner in the Big 12. The electric junior has had documented struggles off of the field, but on the field he has been the Jayhawk's premier skill player for two years running. Without him, Kansas would face Pookacalypse. Pooka has compiled 2186 yards rushing over two seasons with a 6 yard per carry average. Given the overall lack of quality of his surrounding cast, that is no small feat for the small feet of the 5-9, 170-pound runner. Pooka has owned Texas over the last two years (a combined 41 carries, 293 yards rushing, 7.1 average,

with touchdowns runs of 57 and 65 yards) largely because of the defense's inability to honor basic edge principles. That should change under new management as Chris Ash will have a plan to make Pooka a shell of himself. Williams is quick with shocking lateral agility, but also holds up quite well between the tackles despite his slight frame. Pooka will be without departed NFL draft pick offensive tackle Hakeem Adeniji, who was often essential in giving Williams the ability to turn the corner. Expect Pooka to continue to be the mainstay of the Kansas running attack while the Jayhwawks work to get him more opportunities in the passing game.

Andrew Parchment and Stephan Robinson return to form a talented pass catching duo. They were unleashed with the midseason advent of the Kansas RPO game and impressed with their ability to separate and make tough catches in the middle of the field. Andrew Parchment sounds like a witness protection alias, the kind a Brooklyn mobster gets before being sent to live in Twin Falls, Idaho, but even the anonymity of Kansas football could not hide his talent level. Tall and smooth, he was talked about as a potential breakout candidate last year and, no paper tiger, Parchment scrolled through Big 12 defenses last year to the tune of 65 catches for 831 yards and 7 touchdowns. Stephan Robinson added 45 catches for 727 yards and 8 touchdowns of his own. He is quick, dynamic and can make defenders look bad when he can face up with a two way go. Both athletes, along with Pooka Williams, form one of the more impressive skill trios in the league. Let's see what the Les Miles Bermuda Shorts Triangle can do.

Weaknesses: Defense, OL, QB

The Jayhawks return only three defensive starters from a unit that surrendered 36.1 points per game last year (42 points per game in the Big 12) and were ranked 111th in advanced defense metrics. For the record, simple defensive metrics did not favor them either. They were ranked dead last in sacks, pressure, and 3rd down defense. It was a nicely balanced deficiency as the Jayhawks surrendered 249.5 yards passing and 225.7 yards rushing per game to their opponents. Every Big 12 opponent but West Virginia had >400 yards of offense at over 6 yards per play against Kansas. And West Virginia had 394. Four different Big 12 opponents eclipsed >500 yards. The Kansas front seven was a disaster and a senior laden secondary proved helpless against Big 12 quarterbacks and receivers without a pass rush. On the year, they only turned over opponents eight total times. Whatever talent they have is largely gone. Indeed, the dirty birds return only 44% of their 2019 production, a metric that places them smoothly at 117th in the nation. Les Miles raided the JUCOs and transfer portal to try to overhaul his flock, but they are missing nine of their top fifteen tacklers from last year. The big guys up front are too slow and the small guys up front are too weak. The linebackers should be passable - Kyron Johnson and Gavin Potter are OK - but the secondary is inexperienced and not particularly good.

The offensive line is in tatters, but offensive coordinator Brent Dearmon will continue installing an innovative RPO heavy offense that will seek to put defenses in conflict by virtue of scheme and the triangle threat of Parchment, Pooka, and Robinson. That will help take the pressure off of the Jayhawk tackles and keep defenses guessing. Good teams will figure it out, or maybe the Jayhawks will just get outscored, but if you are looking for the most likely prospect for a Kansas conference win (or wins), find the teams that cannot pass rush, have a bad defensive coordinator, or simply lack the talent to cover Robinson and Parchment. Dearborn's play action game could shield the big fellas up front a little and allow them to grow into their roles, but they will miss current Cincinnatti Bengal Hakeem Adeniji. For the second straight season, JUCO Thomas MacVittie allegedly projects as the starting quarterback. The pro style MacVittie is a 6-5, 225 pounder who transferred in from Pittsburgh after a thriving JUCO season. MacVittie was supposed to start last year, but was beaten out in camp by Carter Stanley. Word out of Lawrence is that Les Miles favors the leadership of junior Miles Kendrick and he could actually be their opening game starter. Miles praised Kendrick for having "all kinds of ball skill and hand talent." What exactly this means in the Les-icon is up for debate, but he may be hitting on him?

Texas Christian University

Gary Patterson (20th year)
Defensive Background

2019 RECORD	3 YEAR TREND	5 YEAR TREND
5-7	23-16	40-25

RETURNING STARTERS	OFFENSE	DEFENSE
12	5	7

Last Meeting: TCU- 37, Texas-27 Gary Patterson has won 6 of his last 8 games against Texas and 5 of his last 6. The Frogs had a good game plan in Fort Worth that Texas could not match. Sam Ehlinger was an unimpressive 22 of 48 for 321 yards, throwing four interceptions to go with two passing touchdowns. Texas ran the ball adequately, but was never able to lean on it or marry it to the Longhorn passing game in a disjointed offensive effort. Duvernay and Johnson had big days in the box score, but it was an inefficient passing performance overall as Texas receivers and Ehlinger found themselves far too often on the wrong page. The second half was an offensive disaster. The Texas defense could not handle true freshman quarterback Max Duggan who threw for 273 yards at over 10 yards per attempt and added another 72 yards rushing. Duggan totaled 3 touchdowns and it was, by far, the young true freshman's best performance of the season. Duggan hit big downfield throws of 51 and 44 yards, respectively, in addition to several key opportunistic scrambles and option runs. Texas lost the battle of turnovers, penalties, and preparation. That will usually result in a road loss against Gary Patterson.

Overview

With a 172-70 record at TCU entering his 20th season, Patterson has more experience rebounding than a prime Charles Barkley. He last did it most dramatically in 2013, taking a disappointing 4-8 bunch and transforming them into 12-1 Big 12 champions the following season. That 2013 team lost four games by three points or less before going on their 2014 revenge tour. Last year's TCU team lost six games by a touchdown or less. The 2013 team featured a young, erratic, turnover-prone dual threat quarterback named Trevone Boykin. The 2019 Horned Frogs featured a young, erratic, turnover-prone dual threat quarterback named Max Duggan. The following year, Boykin threw for 3900 yards and ran for over 700. You get the drift. This is not predictive, but merely pointing out that young quarterbacks can get better and good coaches have a knack for bouncing back. Patterson's accomplishments in Fort Worth are unimpeachable and he has outcoached more than his share of Longhorn staffs, but he has not reached program highs as often as he used to. Since 2012 - encompassing TCU's eight years in the Big 12 - Patterson has gone 39-33 in conference play. Over the last four years, he is 18-18 with three of those four years posting losing conference records. Sprinkled into that eight-year mix are three Top 10 finishes, but TCU has been more up and down than a Catholic mass.

Former TCU co-offensive coordinator Doug Meacham rejoins current offensive coordinator Sonny Cumbie in Fort Worth along with Patterson pal Jerry Kill (the former Minnesota head coach). Jerry Kill has been appointed "the head coach of the offense." Not offensive coordinator. The head coach of the offense. He will coach the offensive coaches and see to the total performance of that unit across all positions. Sonny Cumbie will be the coordinator, Meacham will coach inside receivers, and everyone will share ideas. Their main task will be leveling up the offense from the 2019 unit that finished 82nd in the national rankings by progressing sophomore quarterback Max Duggan. Kill's new role will also free Patterson to spend most of his time on the defense, where he will be a pig in slop. Even with heavy losses to the NFL draft, the defense should be on point: the Frogs have finished 1st or 2nd in Big 12 defense for six years straight. They are too program sound to simply fall off of the ledge defensively despite ranking only 64th nationally in returning production. The Frog defense has struggled to handle the best Big 12 passing attacks, but who hasn't?

Most disconcerting for the Purple Toad fanbase is that in the off-season, Gary Patterson recorded a country album. That's right. A country album. Songs like "Swamp Ass Slacks Kinda Feel Nice", "Mah Baby Loves Mah Belly Armrest", and "I'm All Pink Cuz That Sonofabitch Threw A Flag" are the poignant anthems of a generation. Those songs may not actually be on the album, but your money only earns you the best preview on the market, not the right to torture me by forcing a listen. The bigger takeaway is this: when head coaches start recording country albums, indulging hobbies, or learning the names of their children, decline is just around the corner.

Strengths- S, LB, QB(?)

The Frogs have the best safety duo in the league. Junior Trevon Moehrig (6-2, 210) was 1st Team All Big 12 last year and allowed just 2 of 17 contested balls to be caught while he was in coverage. He forced seven turnovers (4 interceptions, 3 forced fumbles) and was also a consistent tackler, coming in 2nd on the team. The former elite recruit is an outstanding football player and may even project as an early NFL draft entry. His sidekick Ar'Darius Washington is a diminutive, speedy safety who covers a lot of ground, and he even packs a little punch as a tackler (3rd on the TCU team last year). Washington goes 5-8, 180 but he has Honey Badger energy and as a redshirt freshman he allowed only five catches in 265 coverage snaps. Washington also grabbed five interceptions, showing sideline to sideline range and great instincts for jumping routes. They lost third safety

Vernon Scott to the NFL Draft, but they should be just fine replacing him. Moehrig and Washington will likely be joined by La'Kendrick Van Zandt (strong name) or sophomore Nook Bradford (named after an obscure e-reader), who have both seen some game action as TCU's third safety. If cool names are correlated to safety play, TCU may even be more loaded than we think. Sidenote: TCU's roster has the strongest apostrophe game in the Big 12.

Former high school safety turned linebacker Garrett Wallow led the league in tackles with 125 (18 tackles for loss) and he is the prototypical smart, instinctive, agile linebacker that TCU seems to churn out on the regular. Now 6-2, 230, Wallow was a 195-pound high school safety at John Curtis in New Orleans, but TCU added size and strength and - voila! - 1st Team All Big 12 linebacker. The Frogs have no lack of possibilities to flank Wallow in Ben Johnson, Dee Winters, or Wyatt Harris in their 4-2-5 defense. Expect a strong unit, per usual.

Listing quarterback as a strength is a reasonable, if risky, inference that Max Duggan will grow considerably from his rocky true freshman year. TCU's offense put far too much on his plate and a young Duggan had more struggles than he did successes. Duggan threw 15 touchdowns and 10 interceptions, completed only 53.4% of his passes, and averaged a meager 6.1 yards per attempt. He demonstrated real ability as a runner, totaling 555 yards and 6 touchdowns, but he will have to progress significantly as a passer if TCU wants to reverse their 3-6 Big 12 finish from last year. The prospectus is

cautiously optimistic that Duggan will move from a liability to at least a competent quarterback. If so, an improved offense married to TCU's characteristic defensive play should result in a better season.

Weaknesses- CB, OL

The Frogs lost three senior offensive linemen, including NFL draft pick offensive tackle Lucas Niang, in addition to Niang's primary backup. They are counting on redshirt junior Coy McMillon (brother of former Longhorn Jake) and 5th year senior Austin Myers to pace the unit, but they badly need graduate transfer T.J. Storment from Colorado State to come through at one tackle spot. The rest of the offensive line is a wide-open competition. In typical TCU fashion, all of the prospective candidates are redshirts who have been in the program for a while, but there is very little clarity on who will man which spots, with the potential for ongoing shuffling through October. This is the biggest single factor that could submarine TCU's season. Max Duggan's mobility will be called on early and often to bail out his offensive line while they work through their growing pains.

Jeff Gladney will be missed at cornerback. Gladney had been a mainstay since 2016 and his skills will not be matched by anyone on the current roster. TCU does not lack raw talent, but this bunch is inexperienced and has not been developed sufficiently. Kee'yon Stewart had six starts as a freshman, but had some struggles due to simply physical immaturity (he is around 165-170 pounds). Tre'Vius Hodges-Tomlinson, nephew of LaDanian Tomlinson, will also vie for a spot at cornerback, and a shot at the title at the preseason Horned Frog apostrophe tournament. He goes around 170 as well. Unlike his smaller peers, Noah Daniels - who missed last season with an injury - is back and he brings rare size and physicality to the position at 6-0, 205. The Frogs do not have the depth or front-line quality they are accustomed to here. Expect coverage help from their elite safeties.

Defensive line could be listed here given what TCU lost to graduation and the NFL Draft, but TCU's ability to consistently restock this position with undersized speedy defensive ends and high motor defensive tackles suggests that Patterson will figure it out. Senior defensive tackle Corey Bethley will provide experience (25 starts in his career) and stability, but look out for defensive end Ochuan Mathis to be a potential breakout star. The redshirt sophomore checks a lot of the boxes for a successful pass rusher in Patterson's system and he has the length (6-5, 245) and quickness to be a major contributor.

Iowa State University
Matt Campbell (5th year)
Offensive Background

2019 RECORD	3 YEAR TREND	5 YEAR TREND
7-6	**23-16**	**29-34**

RETURNING STARTERS	OFFENSE	DEFENSE
13	**5**	**8**

Last Meeting: Iowa State- 23, Texas- 21 The Cyclones led 20-7 before the Longhorn offense (and headsets) woke from their reverie to stage a furious comeback, eventually leading 21-20 in the late 4th quarter. With a chance to deliver the coup de grace with the ball and 4:00 left on the clock, Texas laid up and punted, allowing Iowa State to drive for a game winning 36-yard field goal by Iowa State kicker Connor Assalley. Brock Purdy was good, going 30 off 48 for 354 yards and two touchdowns while Breece Hall provided 101 hard fought rushing yards. Sam Ehlinger threw for a mistake free 273 yards and 3 touchdowns in the loss as the Longhorn offense only managed 54 rushing yards. It was a frustrating and preventable road loss for a Longhorn team that played hard, but stumbled too late into a successful offensive game plan, and then lacked the courage to stick with it. Jamison led the Horns with 9 tackles and an interception from his cornerback position while Joseph Ossai added several quarterback pressures and 9 tackles of his own. DeMarvion Overshown flashed in a handful of snaps, notching two tackles for loss and a nice hit on Purdy.

Overview

Matt Campbell has strung together three consecutive winning seasons at Iowa State after a tough 3-9 debut. That winning season streak was a feat last achieved by Earle Bruce between 1976-1978. There are dry spells and then there is wandering the Sahara Desert with a canteen full of dust. Iowa State has wandered so long in the wastelands that it is hard to fully express what Campbell's winning ways have meant to the Cyclone fanbase. Now the question being asked in Ames is even more provocative: can Iowa State move from a scrappy program playing second fiddle to big brother Iowa to a Big 12 champion? Though the Cyclones return a middling level of production from last year (ranked 52nd in FBS), they also return an elite quarterback, a workhorse runner, the Big 12's best tight end duo, and a sound defense. Matt Campbell is also now all in on throwing it around with his talented quarterback. The Ethanol Raid Cyclones threw for over 311 yards per game and averaged 6.5 yards per play, trading in blue collar ball control for the white collar wide open. Overall, the Cyclones finished 22nd nationally on offense and 43rd on defense. If they can creep those metrics up and take advantage of a distorted college football season that will prioritize coaching consistency and the ability to make do with less, areas where Campbell already excels, the Cyclones could very well match last year's Baylor transformation from nice rebuild story to conference Cinderella.

To do it, they will have to find some answers in the trenches, develop a receiver or two, and channel their inner road warrior sufficiently to take down Oklahoma State or Texas away from Ames, while taking care of the Sooners when they travel to corn country (Iowa State lost to Oklahoma 42-41 in Norman last year). Of course, no farming school can reduce their season to single game siloes. The team that lost to Kansas State last year will have to show up every week. There is also the question of total program talent level for a team that got blown out 33-9 by Notre Dame in the Camping World Bowl, but Iowa State also lost four games last year by a grand total of 11 points. They are *right there.*

Strengths- QB, RB, TE, LB, DE

No sophomore slump for Brock Purdy. He exploded in his 2nd year, throwing for 3982 yards, 27 touchdowns, and 9 interceptions. He also displayed his wheels as the Cyclones 2nd leading rusher with 249 yards, scoring 8 touchdowns on the ground, primarily as a red zone running threat. Purdy completed 65.7% of his throws at a healthy 8.4 yards per attempt and his qualitative level of play was largely excellent. Purdy is highly regarded by NFL GMs and a strong junior season might be his last in Ames. A master of play action, with pump fakes as convincing as Cinemax late night fare, Purdy did not really have a true #1 wide receiver last year - four different Cyclone pass catchers totaled between 600-900 yards receiving - so he should be OK spreading the ball around. Losing the toughness and reliability of leading pass catcher Deshaunte Jones and the chain-moving power of big La'Michael Pettway will be felt though. The long speed of Tariqe Milton is back (35-722) and the Iowa State coaches respect the solidity of Sean Shaw (caught 5 touchdowns in 2019) and the potential of Landen Akers. They also like incoming JUCO Xavier Hutchinson, 6-3, 205, to fill Pettway's role.

Unlike most Big 12 attacks, Purdy will not need to rely entirely on his wide receiver corps. That's because 4th year junior Charlie Kolar is the best tight end in the Big 12. The 6-6, 250-pound Zach Ertz clone has a massive catch radius, moves like a big wide receiver, dominates smaller defensive backs with his size, and runs away from linebackers that can match his physicality. Last year, he had 51 catches for 697 yards, 7 touchdowns, gathered 32 first downs, and made 11 contested catches. It is no coincidence that Iowa State's worst offensive performances came at season's end against Kansas State and Notre Dame, games where Kolar was held to 4 scoreless total catches for 48 yards. The wealth of Cyclone riches at tight end does not end with Kolar. Chase Allen caught 17 balls for 167 yards and two touchdowns last year and you can bet that Iowa State will feature the 6-7, 250-pound Allen in combination with Kolar. Go small and Iowa State might hammer the ball with Breece Hall. Go big and the linebackers may have to cover Allen and Kolar in space. Look for Iowa State's tight end combo to combine for 85+ catches and double-digit touchdowns. The Texas defense will be glad to have defenders like Adimora, Foster, and Overshown to help answer some of the questions that the big Cyclone tight ends will ask the defense.

Breece Hall proved very capable as a freshman runner and receiver last year. In 8 starts, the four-star recruit from Wichita totaled 897 yards rushing and grabbed 23 passes for 252 yards. His ten touchdowns led the Cyclones and the now sophomore will be Iowa State's 2020 workhorse, spelled by capable reserve Johnnie Lang. Like David Montgomery before him, Hall has a diverse skill set that is still growing, but unlike Montgomery, he is a 4.45 40 runner. Add in his hands and feel for the passing game and Purdy will have yet another chess piece to move around the board. Hall's ground game success will rely heavily on Iowa State's ability to replace a departed veteran offensive line and their ability to create leverage outside with their tight ends.

Iowa State continues their tradition of fundamental linebacking play, even with the departure of preview favorite and leading tackler Marcel Spears. 6-4, 245-pound Mike Rose, a former freshman All-American, mans up in the middle and he is a pleasure to watch play the game. Despite layering on thirty pounds since his starting freshman season, Rose is still an instinctive easy mover who moves around in pads as well as he moves around in shorts. He is quite capable in coverage as well. O'Rien Vance is his explosive sidekick. The 6-2, 245-pounder is an excellent blitzer, racking up 6.5 sacks last year. He is not as sophisticated an off-ball linebacker as Rose, but he brings violence of action. 6-1, 230-pound Jake Hummel rounds out the trio and the key reserve notched 36 tackles and an interception last year, getting heavy rotation as the primary back-up at nearly every linebacker spot. Nothing has changed at linebacker for the Cyclones.

The Cyclones also return edge defending pass rusher JaQuan Bailey (18.5 career sacks, 31.5 tackles for loss) who secured a redshirt last season after breaking his leg a few games into the season. Before that injury, the 6-2, 260-pound defensive end had started 37 consecutive games for the Cyclones, earning All-Big 12 Honors in 2018. If he is fully back, the Cyclones have a real impact player in their front four. They also return Will McDonald, a lanky 6-4, 230-pound speed rusher who notched 6 sacks after moving to defensive end from linebacker in midseason. McDonald is a talented athlete with both a basketball and track and field pedigree. As the redshirt sophomore grows into his body and the role, he could be a difference maker. Physical Zach Petersen (6-5, 270) led the defensive line in tackles from his strongside defensive end position and he is a solid run stopper who could benefit from the attention that Bailey and McDonald will elicit on passing downs. The Cyclones might want to explore ways to get those three gentlemen on the field all at once. Iowa State defensive coordinator Jon Heacock has made a name for himself as an innovator with his dime-based defenses. He should consider this his next iteration.

Weaknesses- OL, DT, Turnover creation

The first offensive line featuring Campbell only recruits will try to replace four lost starters who surrendered a Big 12 low 14 sacks and were the best in the league at preventing tackles for loss. The departed offensive line was not dominating, but they were veterans with plenty of scars and experience. They also rarely busted assignments. One of the primary reasons they drilled Oklahoma's stunt-heavy defense for 7 yards per play and 27 second half points. Center Colin Newell (14 career starts) and left guard Trevor Downing (12 starts last year) have starting experience and will be called upon to anchor an otherwise young unit that will be starting over from scratch at tackle, right guard, and much of their two-deep. Campbell has stated emphatically that this offensive line will be his most physically talented at Iowa State, but they lack cohesion, and they have a lot to shake out. There will be a feeling out process. It is also worth noting that in five Iowa State losses last season, they averaged 67.2 yards rushing. Several of those losses were quite competitive so this was not simply a matter of them abandoning the run and trying to play catch-up. They did run the ball effectively at Oklahoma, but simply got outscored. Iowa State only turned it over 16 times all season, but 9 of those turnovers occurred in the five losses where they could not get traction in the ground game. Breaking in a new redshirt freshman and redshirt sophomore starting tackle duo is never easy and Brock Purdy's quick release and mobility will help their cause, but higher-level defenses that can contain Purdy and squeeze the pocket will give them some problems.

The loss of defensive tackles Ray Lima and Jamahl Johnson will be felt if the Cyclones can't think a bit more expansively about solutions inside. Both were tough guys that gave the Cyclones the ability to go small behind them without losing the line of scrimmage. The duo did not make many plays in the backfield and run-stopping interior defenders are not exactly the most coveted asset in the Big 12, but their role was primarily to act as offensive line attractants to free up the Iowa State linebacking corps, allowing Iowa State to play undermanned up front, devoting more personnel and alignment to coverage. Rather than just replacing them with inferior replacements, Iowa State might consider spinning down Zach Peterson from defensive end and get as many of their talented defensive ends on the field as possible. They take a hit on size, but they would be quicker, have more pass rushers, and their linebacking corps and secondary is physical enough to hold up.

Though the Cyclones will return 4 of 5 defensive back starters, including all-conference safety Greg Eisworth and the talented Lawrence White, they did a poor job of playing the ball in the air last year. In 13 contests, the defensive backs combined for four interceptions on 441 opponent passing attempts. Two of those picks came against Louisiana Monroe. A less than 1% interception ratio is awful, effectively failing to threaten offenses with the most important downside risk of throwing the ball. To their credit, this group will stick their noses in there and do not lack for physicality, but whatever praise they get in pass coverage should also be distributed to an Iowa State linebacking corps that has consistently performed well as pass defenders. The Cyclone defensive backs are not a weakness per se, but they need to perform better in one of their primary taskings.

Oklahoma State University

Mike Gundy (16th year)
Offensive Background

2019 RECORD	3 YEAR TREND	5 YEAR TREND
8-5	25-14	45-20

RETURNING STARTERS	OFFENSE	DEFENSE
19	9	10

Last meeting: Texas- 36, Oklahoma State- 30 A close, entertaining game saw Texas pull away late, with the Cowboys cutting the game to six in the final 1:37 of the game. Brandon Jones and Jake Smith both fumbled punts in Texas territory that turned into two Oklahoma State touchdowns. Fortunately, Sam Ehlinger was lights out in one of the best Texas offensive performances of the year. Sam went 20 of 28 for 281 yards and four touchdowns and an interception and also added 70 yards on 10 carries, including a 29-yard scamper. The conventional Texas running game also got after it, as Keaontay Ingram notched 114 yards on 21 carries. His longest run was 16 yards, but he consistently ripped off 4-10-yard gains that kept Texas ahead of the chains and the Cowboys guessing. Brennan Eagles caught one ball for a 73-yard touchdown, while Devin Duvernay caught 12 balls for 108 yards underneath. Joseph Ossai responded to getting some edge snaps, racking up 2 tackles for loss and a sack. Caden Sterns made 12 tackles, 10 of them solo efforts. Reserve safety Montrell Estell was pressed into action and he responded with 9 tackles and an interception that he brought back for 37 yards. Chris Brown also added a pick to go with his 6 tackles. Oklahoma State runner Chuba Hubbard got his 121 yards and 2 touchdowns, but it took 37 carries to get there and the sprinter was held to a longest run of 13 yards. Tylan Wallace was held to 83 yards receiving, a considerable improvement over the 10 catch, 220-yard, 2 touchdown performance he put on Texas in 2018. Spencer Sanders was dangerous to both teams, throwing for 268 yards and running for 109 yards, and demonstrating incredible elusiveness in the pocket, but he also threw two interceptions and had a fumble. The Texas offensive line showed up in a big way, allowing only 3 tackles for loss and surrendering virtually no pressure on Ehlinger. Without a pair of special teams miscues, Texas likely wins going away. Unfortunately, the win came at a cost: Marcus Tillman, Josh Thompson,

Jalen Green, and Caden Sterns all sustained significant injuries.

Overview

Mike Gundy has gone 129-64 in his fifteen seasons at Oklahoma State. He has had only one losing season - his first. Gundy has recorded a half dozen 10+ win seasons and had eight Top 25 finishes. He turns over coordinators like Henry VIII went through wives, has won with every type of quarterback and spread offense imaginable, and grew a trademark mullet that is a gift to us all. For some context to fully understand what Gundy has done in Stillwater, the great Jimmy Johnson went 29-25-3 at Oklahoma State and got out of there to Miami at his first opportunity. Pat Jones won some games coaching Barry Sanders and Thurman Thomas (and Mike Gundy) in the old Big Eight and then strung together six consecutive losing seasons (18-45-3 en total) when those players expired their eligibility and Hart Lee Dykes started talking to NCAA investigators. Les Miles went 28-21 and then sought greener pastures to LSU, his season high water mark a 9-4 record. Gundy is indisputably the most successful coach in Oklahoma State history and he has remained at his alma mater despite some attractive suitors. Now, with 19 starters returning from a 8-5 team bursting with elite talent at several key positions and solid depth across the board, he finds himself poised to break free of a two year stretch of mediocrity and get back to the apogee of Cowboy glory - his 12-1 2011 team that finished ranked 3rd in the country. The Cowboys are top shelf 2020 Big 12 title contenders.

But God and fishing t-shirts laugh at the plans of men. Gundy found himself embroiled in controversy when star running back Chuba Hubbard threatened not to play unless program changes were made. Originally sparked by Gundy wearing a news organization's t-shirt, much more bubbled to the surface. Without getting too lost in the details, Gundy's supposed aloofness, lack of player advocacy, ego, and disconnection from his charges fractured the Cowboy program. Either the Cowboys will work through it and fulfill their potential, or it will hang over the year like a dark cloud and degrade the potential for a special Cowboy season. No team in the Big 12 has a better potential upside.

Strengths: RB, WR, LB, QB, OL

Last year, the preview predicted that Chuba Hubbard was the best bet to win the 2019 Big 12 rushing title despite gaining only 740 yards in 2018. The prospectus even boldly predicted that Hubbard would amass 1750+ yards from scrimmage and 18 touchdowns. Somehow still undersold it. The All-American redshirt junior ran for 2094 yards and 21 touchdowns while adding another 198 yards receiving. The explosive Hubbard had 15 runs of 30+ yards and 7 runs of 50+. He was the premier breakaway running threat in all of college football. The sprinter not only demonstrated constant game-breaking ability, but also excellent durability, totaling 332 touches from scrimmage. He also forced 70 missed tackles and ran for 1185 additional yards after first contact. So what Hubbard gained after the first defender hit him would have still won the Big 12 running back rushing title. So, yes. Hubbard is amazing. And he is back. That he is back is surprising given his 200-pound frame and the finite tread that exists on every runner's tires, but that's a discussion for Chuba and his agent.

Tylan Wallace lost a good portion of the 2019 season to a non contact ACL tear in October, but still managed to grab 53 balls for 903 yards and 8 touchdowns. Before he went down, Wallace was averaging well over 100 yards receiving per game. In 2018, Wallace was probably the most feared wide receiver in the league, totaling 1491 yards on 86 catches and 12 touchdowns. If healthy, Wallace is the best wide receiver in the Big 12. His combination of football speed, route running, and ability after the catch is non-pareil. The added complication for Wallace and his future is that his brother Tracin had to quit football due to multiple ACL tears. Why mention that? Because Tracin is Tylan's twin brother. Senior Dillon Stoner is a nice complementary piece and he has been a fixture in the Cowboy offense for three years running. He has 149 catches in his Oklahoma State career for 1805 yards and 12 touchdowns. Junior Braydon Johnson is not as experienced as Stoner, but he is one of the fastest Cowboys on the team. He averaged 21.3 yards per catch on 23 receptions and scored four touchdowns. 6-5, 230-pound LSU transfer Dee Anderson will join the Pokes and the Texas native is a physical player with top-notch straight-line speed. Oklahoma State has the athletes outside. If Wallace is back 100%? This could be an all-time great Cowboy offense.

Last year, redshirt sophomore Spencer Sanders demonstrated jaw-dropping upside, how-could-you-throw-that downside, and sustained a season-ending injury late in the year (broken thumb) that forced the Cowboys to start Dru Brown the remainder of the season. When Sanders went down, Oklahoma State was 7-3. They finished 1-2 without him, including a frustrating 24-21 loss to Texas A&M in the bowl game. The Big 12 Offensive Freshman of the Year is back after throwing for 2065 yards at a healthy 8.4 yards per attempt along with 16 touchdowns and 11 interceptions. Sanders is also an extremely elusive runner, totaling 628 yards. The 6-1, 200-pound quarterback was an elite player at Denton Ryan before sustaining season ending injuries and that pedigree was evident in several big performances. His talent is not in question. Now it is just a matter of progress. The 3rd year sophomore, surrounded by tremendous weapons, is poised for a breakout year. He will be backed up by freshman Shane Illingworth.

Right tackle Teven Jenkins goes 6-6, 320 and the 5th year senior is an underrated player with NFL ability. He did not allow a sack last year. His left tackle counterpart Dylan Galloway (14 career starts) retired due to accumulated injuries in early July, leaving a hole in the Cowboys offensive front. Inside, the Cowboys will start a 6-6, 340-pound run blocking road grater in Josh Sills, the transfer from West Virginia. He started 24 games there and was 2nd Team All Big 12 as a sophomore. His mullet game is powerful as well. Redshirt sophomore Bryce Bray holds down the other guard job and he is a competent multi-tool who has earned starts at tackle, center, and guard. Center Ry Schneider goes 6-3, 325 and the 5th year Oklahoma native is a former walk-on who ascended up the depth chart with a surprise start as a sophomore against West Virginia that turned into several more starts and heavy rotational play last year. Oklahoma State's offensive line is experienced and fairly talented.

Oklahoma State returns 12 of their top 13 tacklers from a defense that finished 61st nationally. Their most prolific tacklers were linebackers Malcolm Rodriguez and Amen Ogbongbemiga. The speedy 6-1, 230-pound Ogbongbemiga showed star quality, totaling 100 tackles, 5 sacks, 15.5 tackles for loss, and grabbed an interception. Not bad. Can we get an Amen? Rodriguez was Oklahoma State's leading tackler, totaling 103 stops, 7 tackles for loss, and an interception of his own. Rodriguez is undersized at 5-11, 210 but the former safety also brings versatility and coverage ability.

Weaknesses- DL

Sophomore defensive end Trace Ford is the potential class of the bunch. He showed real pass rushing ability as a true freshman with 29 tackles and 3 sacks in six starts. Defensive tackle Israel Antwine is a 295-pound space eater with 20 career starts. He is fine against the run and a negligible pass rusher. Cameron Murray will play inside beside him and he had 30 tackles and 3.5 sacks in 13 starts last year. He is an active player, but has not been, to date, a difference maker. Perhaps that will change. Finally, defensive end Tyler Lacy started 10 games last year but the 6-4, 275-pound strongside defensive end showed very little pass rushing ability. This unit is average and unless Ford can put together a major breakout season from his weak side defensive end position, Oklahoma State's ability to get to the passer will be negligible without constantly blitzing their linebackers and safeties.

The Oklahoma State secondary is not a weakness across the board - cornerback Rodarius Williams is a multi-year starter, and sophomore safety Kolby Harvell-Peel is a real player, but the dropoff from departed cornerback AJ Green will likely be felt, even if the job is manned by converted starting safety Jarrick Bernard.

Big XII Strength of Schedule Rankings
according to SportsBettingDime

	CONF RANK	NAT'L RANK	SOS TOTAL
Kansas	1	18	129.51
West Virginia	2	21	116.39
TCU	3	24	109.85
Baylor	4	33	92.93
Kansas State	5	37	80.02
Oklahoma	6	38	78.73
Texas	7	39	77.19
Iowa State	8	46	57.82
Oklahoma State	9	49	55.26
Texas Tech	10	52	47.86

SBD formula based upon opponent's returning starters, returning production, recruiting rankings, transfers, estimated Vegas win totals.

The Big 12's worst teams do not get to play themselves, which bolsters their schedule strength. Similarly, the best teams cannot play themselves, creating a natural hit on their rankings. That's the paradox of schedule strength in the Big 12's round robin conference format.

The non-conference slate is another matter. The Big 12 has some terrific games and a few that qualify as intriguing. The most important non-conference games for the Big 12 are headlined by early Big 12/SEC matchups. Specifically, Texas at LSU and Tennessee at Oklahoma. Winning those two contests would be a significant blow to SEC efforts down the road to get two or even three teams into the College Football Playoff. Baylor- Ole Miss in Houston doesn't quite have the panache of the aforementioned, but their battle will be intriguing. Iowa State travels to Iowa where the Hawkeyes have won the last five in a row. A victory there would provide an important confidence boost for the

Cyclones. TCU will have a defensive battle with Cal in Berkeley, assuming California has not canceled football, competition, and any sports with balls (interpret that as you wish). Whoever gets to 20 points first wins. TCU also travels to SMU seeking vengeance (and the coveted Iron Skillet Trophy) for last year's 41-38 loss to the Ponies. Oklahoma will travel to West Point and all right-thinking Americans will be pulling for the improbable upset. Other interesting non-cons include West Virginia at Florida State and the Mountaineers hosting Texas-slayer Maryland. A tip of the hat to West Virginia for scheduling 11 legitimate P-5 schools. A Bronx cheer to Kansas State, who will play Vanderbilt, Buffalo, and North Dakota (no, not dangerous North Dakota State, but the former Fighting Sioux, now Hawks, who were 1-5 on the road last year).

Of course, no Big 12 team can match the scheduling cynicism of the Texas A&M Aggies. Texas A&M boasts the 75th best strength of schedule in college football. Highlighted by a ridiculous non-conference slate (Abilene Christian, Colorado, North Texas, Fresno State), complemented by a favorable SEC East draw (Vandy, South Carolina), and given the low level of play expected from SEC West mates Arkansas, Ole Miss, and possibly Mississippi State, that virtually guarantees a nine-win regular season. Despite all evidence to the contrary, expect them to be granted the media's blanket assumption of a brutal SEC schedule.

Ranking Texas Schedule Difficulty

EASIEST TO HARDEST

UTEP

South Florida

@Kansas

West Virginia

Baylor

@Texas Tech

@Kansas State

TCU

Iowa State

@LSU

@Oklahoma State

Oklahoma (Dallas)

Remember, in assessing schedule difficulty, when and where Texas plays their opponent matters. This is not a pure power ranking of each opponent on a neutral field played under perfect conditions in the middle of October. The Longhorns are happy to have LSU in the second week of September and, trap games notwithstanding, it's nice to catch Kansas State before their offensive line can gel, even if on the road. Getting Baylor in late October increases the chances that Texas might see a different signal caller than Brewer. Playing Oklahoma State in Stillwater in a short week turnaround after a brawl with Iowa State is decidedly suboptimal. One can get a bit carried with this - football is football -

and every team has their seasonal ebbs and flows, but it is a factor.

Last year, the preview offered that 2019 Longhorn season upside boiled down to four contests: @TCU, @Iowa State, Oklahoma, and LSU. Texas went 0-4 in those games. 8-1 in all others. So much for potential upside. They were outplayed and outcoached by TCU and Oklahoma on both sides of the ball, The Longhorn staff played 12th defender against the Longhorn offense in Ames, and Texas lost out on a prime opportunity for a program rallying upset against LSU.

This year, the Big 12 has four clear championship contenders: Oklahoma, Oklahoma State, Texas, and Iowa State. Oklahoma has won five consecutive Big 12 titles and are the default choice for a title until proven otherwise. Anyone expecting a Sooner offensive decline is probably in for a rude awakening. Oklahoma State is loaded with talent and experience, with the most returning starters in the league, and they host the Cyclones and Longhorns at home. The Cowboy program is starting to show some off-the-field cracks though, and that is worth monitoring. Iowa State has good coaching, the potential for a solid defense, and a big-time college quarterback with enough weapons around him. The ball might bounce their way in a season that could be determined simply by which team's starters are in quarantine or which campus blows up with student activism.

Finally, Texas. The conference wildcard. A riddle wrapped in an enigma. The Longhorns may have the most balanced roster in the league and the best depth - a key ingredient in any season, but particularly important in a year where an entire defensive backfield could end up with a two-week time out. Texas has a veteran high-level quarterback and abundant talent at every level of the defense with a new coaching staff ostensibly focused on teaching instead of shortcuts. What's not to like?

Texas also enters the 2020 season full of off-field distractions, seemingly lacking cohesion, with new systems to learn. Deprived of spring practices and with the likely prospect of learning under live fire in September and early October, an early upset loss in Manhattan and Herman going 1-4 to Oklahoma in Dallas could put the Longhorns behind the eight ball before the season even gets going. Conversely, Texas could gain confidence with a close gutty win against LSU in Baton Rouge, take their practice reps against an outmatched UTEP and South Florida, bully Kansas State's inexperienced lines, take down a rookie quarterback in the Red River Shootout, scythe through the middling middle of the schedule, and have it all come down to back-to-back games against the Cyclones and Cowboys.

An 8-1 Longhorn conference finish, a Big 12 title win, and a playoff berth does not require that much imagination. Conversely, neither does a dispiriting 5-4 conference underachievement and another 8-5 season of national irrelevance. Texas has a clear path to the Big 12 title. It runs through the Cotton Bowl, Stillwater, and at home against Iowa State.

2020 Big XII Conference Predictions

Oklahoma	8-1
Oklahoma State	7-2
Texas	7-2
Iowa State	6-3
TCU	4-5
Kansas State	3-6
Texas Tech	3-6
Baylor	3-6
West Virginia	3-6
Kansas	1-8

Conference Trends

Every year the NFL Draft offers a hard dose of demographic reality to Big 12 conference apologists (yes, there still are some) and 2020 was no different. However, for the second time since the 2012 Big 12 conference realignment the conference is not dead last of the major P-5 conferences in per capita draft ratio. It's second to last, finishing just above the ACC for the second straight year. Before we roll out the ticker tape, know that the Big 12 was between the AAC and beleaguered Pac 12 in average NFL draft quality per team. The AAC features teams like Tulane, Tulsa and East Carolina, and the Pac 12 thinks hacky sack is a contact sport. The SEC and upper tiers of the Big 10 can barely see the Big 12 in their rearview mirrors.

Here are the numbers by conference:

NFL Draft Picks by Conference

	DRAFT PICKS	AVG /TEAM
SEC	63	4.50
Big 10	48	3.53
PAC 12	32	2.67
ACC	27	1.80
Big 12	21	2.10
AAC	17	1.42
M West	10	0.83
Conf USA	10	0.73
Remainder	27	-

The SEC's dominance continues. LSU had fourteen players drafted, five in the first round. Alabama also had nine players drafted, including four first round selections. SEC teams will continue to argue to state of Texas recruits that the "The Big 12 is the minor leagues." And then show some clips of the LSU-Oklahoma playoff game.

The Big 10 had an outstanding draft year, powered heavily by Michigan and Ohio State. While the Pac 12 is limping badly perceptually, it is resilient from a pure talent standpoint. If USC can ever get squared away and

Arizona State continues its talent rise, they can match the success of their northwestern brethren and start to change the narrative. ACC talent decline continues to puzzle. It used to be the shadow SEC, churning out tons of NFL talent. Now they are closer to Conference USA than they are to the Big 10. Texas fans who want to leave the Big 12 and blithely offer the ACC as a solution are simply not paying attention on a number of different levels. The ACC saw a massive drop in draft prospects from its historical norm for the second straight year. It is Clemson and everyone else, and most of everyone else cares primarily about college basketball and lacrosse. Maybe Mack at Carolina will help.

While not a Power 5 conference, the AAC had a nice little year putting 17 players into the draft. Houston, Temple, and Memphis continue to quietly serve as useful NFL feeders.

Right now, LSU, Alabama, and Ohio State have better stories to tell in Texas prospect living rooms about putting Texas athletes into the NFL than the Horns do. The only way out is to develop more players into the NFL. A teaching-oriented staff is a positive step in that direction.

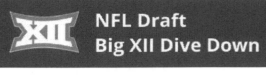

NFL Draft
Big XII Dive Down

	DRAFT PICKS
TCU	5
Baylor	4
Oklahoma	3
Texas	3
West Virginia	2
Texas Tech	2
Kansas	1
Kansas State	0
Iowa State	0
Oklahoma State	0

The Frogs had two 1st rounders (Jeff Gladney, Jalen Reagor) a 2nd rounder (Ross Blacklock), a 3rd rounder (Lucas Niang) and Vernon Scott drafted late. Not bad at all. That yielded a 5-7 record. Not good.

Baylor capped their turnaround season with Denzel Mims, James Lynch, Brayvion Roy, and Clay Johnston all getting selected.

Conference champion Oklahoma had four picks, but they were all quality with Ceedee Lamb and Kenneth

Murray going in the 1st, Jalen Hurts in the 2nd, and Neville Gallimore in the 3rd.

Texas was 4th in league draft output, putting Brandon Jones, Devin Duvernay, and Colin Johnson into the show.

West Virginia had Kenny Robinson and Colton Mckivitz selected.

Texas Tech managed two with Jordyn Brooks and Broderick Washington.

Finally, Kansas offered Hakeem Adeniji as their only contribution.

Iowa State, Oklahoma State, and Kansas State did not have a single player drafted. Iowa State and Oklahoma State's best talent was young. Kansas State had a respectable season exploiting seniority and contrarianism, not raw NFL talent.

It is safe to say that the 2019 Big 12 is not a talent rich league. Alabama and LSU combined had more draftable talent than the entire Big 12. That is not media bias. That is the opinion of 32 NFL teams.

2020 Recruiting Class Overview

The 2019 class was defined by out of state recruiting. 14 out of 25 Longhorn signees hailed from outside the borders of the Lone Star state. The highest ratio of out-of-state recruits in school history. Longhorn coaches rang up frequent flyer miles to Florida, Arizona, California, Georgia, Louisiana, Iowa, and Missouri, while collecting a Top 5 nationally ranked class. That class was eroded by tragic health issues (Derrian Brown, De'Gabriel Floyd) and a touch of West Coast flakiness (Bru McCoy), but it was a strong effort nonetheless.

The 2020 recruiting class was a pivot to staycations and Mama's home cooking. Every single member of the 20-man class, save running back Bijan Robinson, hails from the great state of Texas. That native bias did not come at the expense of quality - the relatively small class still ranked in the Top 10 nationally and on a per player average basis, graded out as #6 overall. Perhaps the most encouraging thing about this 2020 class is that few of them will be needed to play early, assuming pandemic or social unrest does not weigh in too destructively. It is also further encouraging that, consistent with Herman's prior Texas classes, rare is the moment when you evaluate a prospect and think,"Weird. I don't get it." That has not always been the case with Herman's predecessors.

The very concept of impact freshmen is often as much a sign of a depleted unbalanced roster as elite freshmen arriving on campus and dominating. If you are a longtime Texas fan, there is a good chance that you have lived through multiple cycles of savior recruiting classes pressed too soon into action instead of being given reasonable developmental timelines. A two deep full of eighteen year olds does not mean your latest class is one for the ages. It means the Horns are in trouble.

The good news for 2020 Texas is that the Longhorns will largely feature a roster without glaring holes, act of God disclaimers inserted here, and given 2020 to date, we can probably expect an alien invasion and the semi-dormant volcano under Yellowstone to start spewing lava. The precocious 2020 freshman that finds his way to the two deep will need to be a very good football player to get on the field for anything more than special teams. That is good program news.

By contrast, if the talent level of a freshman is so significant that he is beating out quality established veterans, or even forcing an alteration of offensive plans or schemes, now you are in true impact freshman territory. We know who these players are: Ricky Williams, Roy Williams, Derrick Johnson, just to name a few. Could Bijan Robinson be that good? Maybe. But let's see him in pads before the coronation.

What about big Alfred Collins? Sure. But he has some pretty good players to beat out first. Is it coincidence that Earl Thomas and Vince Young redshirted while Longhorn football was very good? It is not. The redshirt is not just a developmental tool, it is a reflection of a healthy roster. Tom Herman's program has substantially upgraded the raw talent level on the Longhorn roster.

OFFENSE

Hudson Card	**QB**	**6-2,185**	**Austin, TX**	**4 star**

The former Lake Travis star logged the highest ball velocity measure of any camper at Elite 11 and, on film, the ball leaps out of his hand when he wants to zip it. Card has a 37-inch vertical leap and a 4.06 short shuttle. Those are elite measurements for a defensive back, much less a quarterback. Little wonder that Card was a star wide receiver for the Cavaliers as a sophomore. His weight is not a concern for any if he is capable of getting older, lifting weights, and eating food. Hudson will fill out to 205-210 in short order.

The vertical leap is the premier measure of power display and genetic explosiveness. Card's vertical is not intriguing because it suggests he could hurdle a tackler or kill it at the Fiji Low Hoop tournament. It's a peek under the genetic hood. A diagnostic. It means that he is far more likely to improve or retain speed and athleticism as he gains weight than we ordinary mortals. Card's velocity metrics, despite the skinniest frame at the Elite 11 camp, stems from the same causal root as the twitchiness that allows him to vertical like a NFL cornerback. That rocket arm can get even better while some of his peers, who have had personal trainers and private coaches since junior high, are already maxed out. Card's change of direction compares favorably to Russell Wilson's 4.09 and Johnny Manziel's 4.03 short shuttles at the NFL combine. They are elusive by any standard. Wilson to NFL pass rushers, Manziel to common sense and good taste. Elusiveness is a helpful eraser to have on the offensive pencil. Whether sliding in the pocket, rescuing a play with his feet, or the ability to plant and go upfield instantly, it has a pretty good correlation to real football and what Texas asks its quarterbacks to do.

Ultimately, Card will prove out based on traits we cannot easily measure outside of game action: attributes like anticipation, ball placement, processing speed, and leadership. There were times when Card looked mechanical at Lake Travis, needing to see the receiver open before the ball came out instead of anticipating the break, but this is an area of growth for almost all high school quarterbacks. His senior year was derailed by injury, but Card was an early enrollee and is ready to go.

Ja'Quinden Jackson   QB/ATH   6-2, 220   Dallas, TX   4 star

It is hard not to fall in love with Ja'Quinden after watching just a few frames of his film. Jackson is an assertive alpha dog who offers the impression that he is happy to beat you on the field and shake your hand after, or continue the competition later in the parking lot if you step up to him the wrong way. Jackson has a huge arm, but he lacks refinement. He is more powerful than straight line fast (4.6 40), but his physicality is top notch. He discards arm tacklers like insects. Jackson is not a studied or particularly disciplined quarterback at the stage in his development. He is more on the force of nature side of the equation. At quarterback, his ability to adapt to the nuanced requirements of the college game will be his primary challenge, but his competitiveness, toughness, and fight all check out. Jackson is a good enough athlete to be a potential starter at positions as diverse as linebacker, tight end, or even running back, but Texas coaches should be cautious about a position switch without giving a full developmental hearing to his quarterback skills. Ja'Quinden can blow like a Cat 5 hurricane with the ball in his hands, but his ultimate success at quarterback will be in his ability to harness the breeze. His senior year at Duncanville was derailed by a partial ACL tear, but he is all patched up and ready to roll.

Bijan Robinson   RB   6-0,200   Tucson, AZ   5 star

Longhorn running backs coach Stan Drayton finally landed the big one after playing bridesmaid on several high-profile national running back recruitments. Robinson is a five-star running back who picked the Horns over Ohio State and USC. He was considered one of the Top 15 prospects in the country and 24/7 ranked him as the #1 running back prospect in the nation. His film is fantastic, even if you control for competition that largely looks like bad Texas 3A football. Robinson compiled 7,036 rushing yards and 112 touchdowns in his high school career, with a 13.4 per carry average. That is not a misprint. 13.4 yards per carry. That number is impressive against a Pop Warner team. Robinson gets in and out of his cuts like greased lightning and he has burst when he plants his foot and hits the gas. He also shows consistently good vision and an understanding of where defensive help is coming from. Robinson is a good pass receiver and comparisons to Alvin Kamara are not inapt. Running backs that get in and out of their cuts quickly translate very well one level up. Bijan is an upright runner, which helps him with vision and making wicked cuts, but he'll need to learn to lower his pad level at or near contact when he encounters athletes that aren't from southern Arizona high schools. He will probably learn that lesson the hard way in August. Robinson showed out at national camps among higher level athletes and his list of suitors and the intensity of his national recruitment speaks for itself. He will be one of the few freshmen who could vie for early playing time.

| Troy Omeire | WR | 6-3,210 | Houston, TX | 4 star |

"When the moon hits your eye like a big pizza pie, that's Omeire!"

No apologies for the Dad joke. If the Big Pie or the Big Pizza hits as his nickname, *Thinking Texas Football* demands its cut of name, image, and likeness rights. Troy Omeire may owe an apology to some heartbroken Aggies. He was pledged to Texas A&M, but flipped to Texas late when his recruitment exploded in conjunction with a dominating senior season. Don't worry about the Aggies. Their fanbase handles late flips to Austin with grace and understatement. Omeire's junior film showed a willing blocker, good hands, and a big frame. He created separation with size and solid routes, not necessarily speed. In his senior season, Omeire went to the next level: rag dolling defenders, accelerating through contact like a young Larry Fitzgerald, demonstrating beautiful route breaks, and highlighting a level of explosiveness with the ball in his hands that only could be described as electric. The junior Omeire was a medium floor, medium ceiling possession receiver. The senior Omeire looked like a borderline five-star recruit toying with 6A Texas high school talent. Whatever Omeire added to his water between his junior and senior seasons, we want some. Troy is an early enrollee and his physical maturity and developmental trajectory could absolutely demand playing time as a true freshman. The Longhorns inked a great late-developing talent.

| Kelvontay Dixon | WR | 6-0, 180 | Carthage, TX | 4 star |

Brother of Longhorn running back Keaontay Dixon, Kelvontay led the state champion Carthage Bulldogs to a 16-0 record, catching 73 balls for 1223 yards and 20 touchdowns. Dixon has legitimate track speed and athleticism, having recorded a 10.71 100 meters and winning silver in the 4A Triple Jump. The former Arkansas pledge was a late addition to the class, but he balled in his senior season.

| Dajon Harrison | WR | 5-10, 175 | Hutto, TX | 3 star |

Harrison caught 41 balls for the Hutto Hippos, scoring 10 touchdowns in an injury-shortened senior season. Harrison projects to slot receiver and he has excellent short area quickness. He can flip his hips and accelerate at an elite level. He evokes former New York Jet, TCU Horned Frog, and Hutto Hippo, Jeremy Kerley. He is deadly in the screen game, featuring sharper cuts than a katana. He also flashes as a cornerback prospect and Jay Valai may want to sneak him into a few defensive back drills when Andre Coleman is not looking. The former TCU pledge was a late addition when several Longhorn receiver prospects reversed their pledges, but his recruiting rankings do not accurately reflect his ability level. A late addition and a welcome addition. Be excited that Dajon Harrison is in this class. His quickness is uncommon.

Jake Majors OL 6-3, 285 Prospect, TX 4 star

The prospect from Prospect was a high school tackle, but he projects inside at the next level. Majors shows agile feet that he parlays into favorable positioning with the technical ability to finish a block. Majors shows a good motor and his mobility should translate well on pulls and angling defenders inside. He is not an elite gross measurables athlete and he has an average FBS frame for his projected position. He will have to develop technically and physically so that he is not overwhelmed at the point of attack. His athleticism is subtle and he needs a long dip in the S&C developmental pool to highlight it. Majors needs a redshirt and time to build out his strength base.

Logan Parr OL 6-4, 280 Helotes, TX 4 star

Parr has really nice get-off at the snap of the ball and finishes blocks with tenacity and good foot placement. There is some real nasty and attitude in his game, he is always looking for work, and that will translate well to the next level. His recruitment, like many the other offensive line prospects in this class, is a transition away from the behemoth interior offensive line model. Texas is clearly looking for feet and motors. He will excel in a play action system that features a lot of pulling and heavy use of outside zone run plays. Parr played at multiple spots in high school, but his most likely projection is guard or center. Parr is a high floor prospect.

Jaylen Garth OL 6-5, 285 Port Neches-Grove 4 star

Long-armed, powerful, and physical, Garth looks like a right tackle prospect. He finishes blocks with aggression and nastiness and seems to relish the physical aspects of the game. High-waisted, Garth needs to work to keep his base and weight settled, shoot his hands out, and not lunge against pass rushers. Allows pass rushers into his body at times. That was all an evaluation of his junior film. A knee injury in August of his senior year did him no favors developmentally or in our ability to evaluate his likely improvements. He missed all of 2019. He has a longer developmental trajectory, as much for skill acquisition, as for acquiring more size, weight, and strength. His feet can get messy, but they are not necessarily bad feet - just untrained. The athleticism and attitude check out and, absent senior film, it is possible that Garth has already progressed quite a bit in all facets.

Andrej Karic	**OL**	**6-5, 270**	**Dallas, TX**	**4 star**

Karic is the most intriguing offensive line prospect in the class. Given that he is the lowest rated of the four Texas prospects by various recruiting experts, that demands an explanation. Here it is: growing big framed offensive tackles from a strong athletic base whenever possible is a good idea. Karic is a fine example of that concept. Adding weight and strength to a very athletic young man is the easiest thing to do in sports. Every year professional evaluators miss this obvious point, much to the detriment of their rankings. See Connor Williams. Williams was an athletic "undersized" recruit that this preview advocated for strongly a few years ago, predicting him to be a college star. Karic's senior film raised him late to a consensus low four star, as he demonstrated terrific feet, punch at the point of attack, and a great work rate. Karic also had offers punching above his recruiting service perception: Michigan, USC, Auburn, FSU to name just a few. Those recruiters saw the same film I did. If there is a knock on Karic's upside, and it is a potentially legitimate one, it is a short wingspan. That is predictive of NFL success, but it is not strictly determinative of a college career.

DEFENSE

Alfred Collins	**DL**	**6-5, 285**	**Basdrop, TX**	**4 star**

Perhaps the highest upside signee in the class, Collins checks nearly every box for a defensive line prospect. He racked up 86 tackles and 35 tackles for loss to go with four forced fumbles at Bastrop in his senior season, earning 5A State Defensive Lineman of the Year honors, but it is his athletic traits - both mental and physical - that leap from the film frame. Collins is extremely long, powerful, and plays through the whistle on every play. He also exhibits real athletic awareness and is clearly a quick learner. The basketball standout has great body control, but plays with the physicality of a college wrestler. Collins has already added nearly forty pounds to his frame in a year and, far from detracting from his athleticism, the weight and strength seem to have advanced it. He will play his best football at Texas north of 300 pounds, while still retaining a flat belly and a lot of agility. Alfred's ability to move for his size is stunning and he should project very well to the 3 technique position where his length will muddy quarterback windows and his quickness can create disruption and penetration. Collins checks every box and then adds a few new ones.

| **Vernon Broughton** | **DL** | **6-4, 290** | **Houston, TX** | **4 star** |

Broughton was a highly recruited defensive line prospect for good reason. He has special quickness and explosiveness for his size and possesses the versatility to play in almost any role on a defensive front. Broughton will need to remake his body, but that is actually good news. When a player who has not yet filled out his lower body, or reapportioned his upper body, but can still exhibit elite traits, there is a lot of upside yet untapped. If there is a knock on the big man, it was a middling senior season from a pure production standpoint. Broughton was late to football, preferring basketball, and he is still learning to translate his traits to playmaking. He is a big man with a small man's game - which is both his best attribute and a mindset that he must grow out of. Broughton was a participant in the 2020 Under Armour game and he impressed in practices against the nation's elite. Vernon will bring impressive raw traits to Texas. It will be up to the Horns to shape and form them. Those expecting immediate impact from Broughton may find that he has a longer-term developmental window.

| **Sawyer Gorham-Welch** | **DL** | **6-4, 295** | **Longview, TX** | **3 star** |

Sawyer Gorham-Welch sounds like a progressive alt country band that raps about dirt roads and cutoff jeans shorts, but he is actually an underrated, nasty, highly physical defensive line prospect from state champion Longview. An all-state performer, Gorham-Welch will not be confused with a finesse defender. He is as subtle as a bull in a China shop and exhibits terrific initial pop. While he played a three-man front defensive end position for the Lobos - lining up anywhere from the 4i position to a 7 technique - he projects inside in the Longhorn defense. A position switch to the interior offensive line would also serve him favorably. Every strength he possesses translates well to offensive line play and he would be a plus athlete there. You certainly want no part of SG-W in a phone booth, but he has better short area quickness on the field than casual impressions suggest. Upside comparisons to Baylor's James Lynch are not bad (though SG-W is currently the same weight as Lynch while five years younger), but I see more similarities to former Longhorn defensive tackle James Patton.

Prince Dorbah LB 6-2, 210 Dallas, TX **4 star**

Dorbah was a dominant high school player for a dominant 5A program, tallying 40 sacks and 67 quarterback pressures over the course of his career. Dorbah is also a fine basketball player and his combination of speed and quickness was simply too much for opposing high school offensive linemen. Dorbah actually played a lot of snaps with his hand down at the 4i position for Highland Park and his lack of a clean position projection to college makes him an interesting, if controversial, recruit. Some college recruiters and analysts make the case that he is a dominant edge rusher or an off-the-ball linebacker waiting to happen, still others tag him with the dreaded tweener label. Dorbah is cat quick, can cover ground, and bend. Finding a role for his traits should not be that hard - whether at JACK, Will linebacker, or situational pass rusher - particularly as he fills out to a college playing weight between 235-250.

Xavion Alford S 6-0, 180 Houston, TX **4 star**

Alford missed most of his senior season with a knee injury. Xavion has a high-level football mind and good enough mobility to get his sticky hands where his high football IQ directs him to go. While he has the ability to play nickel or cornerback, that would be a waste of his strengths. He is a classic field or free safety who uses vision, range, and gridiron intellect to snuff out opposing offenses. The Texas defense wants him looking at the quarterback from deep, evaluating route combinations, and then jumping them. Alford is a willing tackler, but needs a lot more strength to hold up in the college game. The early enrollee wants to play immediately and has the capacity to contribute, but Longhorn coaches might want to sell him on the idea that another young free safety named Earl Thomas redshirted as a freshman, and it turned out OK for him.

Jerrin Thompson S 6-1, 180 Lufkin, TX **4 star**

Thompson hits like a skinny ton of bricks. Imagine what he will do when he is walking around at 205. Thompson brings plenty of East Texas attitude to the field but he is more than just an enforcer. He moves very well laterally (4.20 short shuttle) and demonstrates good ability to cover ground under the lights in pads, not just in a testing environment. Like Alford, he has a good football IQ and seems to understand what he is seeing in front of him at a higher level than most athletes at the same age. Thompson could play either of the safety positions and possibly Spur for Chris Ash's defense. While he could certainly contribute as a potential special teams coverage asset, getting him four games of action and a redshirt sounds even better.

Kitan Crawford	CB	5-11, 200	Tyler, TX	4 star

The do-everything athlete from Tyler will play cornerback where the skills he developed as a running back, returner, and receiver will serve him well. A top 25 state of Texas talent, Kitan could play at a number of spots, but cornerback will be the most lucrative. Crawford has recorded a 10.60 100 meters and given his broad, sturdy running back frame, he could be a press coverage monster if he can also keep fluid hips. Crawford was a 1,000 yard rusher in his senior season playing both ways and added another 21 catches as a receiver. He also nabbed three interceptions on defense. Once Crawford has the ability to specialize at cornerback and learn his craft, Texas should have a dynamic ball-hawking outside defender with the physicality to stand up to big wide receivers. Crawford will also provide value as a potential punt and kick returner.

Jahdae Barron	CB	5-11, 175	Austin, TX	4 star

Barron's fortuitous flip from Baylor occurred well after national signing day when Matt Rhule left Waco for the NFL, giving the Longhorns a much-needed second cornerback to complement Kitan Crawford. Barron is a very good cornerback prospect in his own right. The Pflugerville Connally athlete has notched a 10.95 100 meters and is smooth in his back pedal and break. He is a natural corner and a willing tackler on the edge. When Jahdae plants his foot and decides to bring it, he looks like a college cornerback. Jahdae played both ways for Connally and added 673 yards receiving and 6 touchdowns on 41 catches in addition to three interceptions on defense. Specialist high school cornerbacks who only play on defense can be a warning flag with respect to ball skills and both Crawford and Barron rate positively.

Jaden Hullaby	ATH	6-2, 210	Dallas, TX	3 star

The Swiss Army knife from DFW ran for 1181 yards as a junior at Bishop Dunne while grabbing another 33 passes, but played quarterback as a senior for Mansfield Timberview, where he compiled 20 touchdowns and 1st Team All District honors. Hullaby will not play either at Texas. If he plays offense, think Oklahoma's Dmitri Flowers - a pass catching, lead-blocking move TE or H-Back. If linebacker, he has the requisite athleticism to play in the middle or outside, it is really a matter of mental and technical fit and how quickly he takes to it. Hullaby is a fine all-around athlete with great hands and good body control. Give him some time to grow into his body and role.

Jaylan Ford **LB** **6-2, 210** **Dallas, TX** **3 star**

The late flip from Utah was a productive high school player, racking up 142 tackles and 11 tackles for loss as a senior and 105 tackles and 8 tackles for loss as a junior while compiling District MVP honors and two-time All-State selections. He also ran the 110 meter hurdles. Ford has average measurables, but he has a rangy frame to add strength and weight and good football coordination. Ford is a very solid off-the-ball linebacker whose best attribute is a nose for the football. While that would seem to be a basic qualifying attribute for linebacker play, it has been too often missing from the Longhorn program as recruiters have opted for too many statues that lack basic football instincts or the ability to flow to a ball carrier. Ford needs a redshirt and years in the weight room to bring out his best possible use.

The Eyes of Texas are Upon Us

The Eyes of Texas are upon us. Perhaps even the eyes of a nation.

I want to offer my thoughts on what The Eyes of Texas represents to me, and perhaps in so doing, it will speak to some of you. That means more than just highlighting its association with a vile practice that once was, six generations past, but also striking a balance with the song's unifying modern practice. It is the only way to make sense of it and perhaps find some clarity of purpose.

Absent context, our history and the imperfect realizations of our ideals throughout, merely become a tool for an endless series of recriminations against the practices of men long dead. The sad state of affairs for most of human history. If one holds that everything we drink is fetid water sourced from a poisoned historical well; that all progress is illusory, suspect in its origin; any positive growth merely fleeing an original sin, where is that journey taking us?

An African proverb offers wisdom for any journey: "If you want to go quickly, go alone. If you want to go far, go together."

I want to go together.

In practice, though not origin, The Eyes of Texas represents unity. We sing it rapturously with strangers of every possible background, belief system, and identity to mark our victories. We let it ring out defiantly after a loss, with one voice and purpose, reassuring our Burnt Orange tribe that we will endure. I was a young teenager shivering in a miserable cold drizzle as Baylor dismantled a hapless Texas team 50-7 in Memorial Stadium. As the stadium crowd began to thin well before the final gun, I looked over at my father expectantly, the metal bleachers around us protesting the crowd's hard, joyless steps to the exits. "We stay until the Eyes," he said. I nodded. His tone implied that this was fundamental to our character, who we were. We would see this through, good or bad. We must accept setbacks in order to relish the triumphs. If not with equanimity, at least resolve.

Because we were all in it together.

I was ignorant of the song's shameful racist association, as I suspect were the majority of us for most of our lives. It has been reported that the song debuted in 1903 at a campus spirit organization's minstrel show, a practice that was indisputably dehumanizing and dishonorable. The song's presentation, while sadly of its time, should not necessarily degrade our current understanding of it. The song itself is not racist nor is its recent and current practice. Its spirit changed with the community it represents, just as that community changed. Like many of our nation's ideals, it was up to us to expand that proposition to all. Originally sung by an all white student body, it has been, increasingly, for over six decades, sung proudly by a diverse one. Not to mention the many who follow Texas that never attended the school. It cements an association whose only requirement is a shared love for Texas: the school, the state, its pride, and yes, its myth and legend. It has punctuated joyous events beyond athletics: graduations, weddings, the birth of a child - and it has echoed hauntingly and solemnly across manicured grass pillared by stone epitaphs and remembrances.

It is iconic, imbues common identity, and fosters powerful solidarity. I do not want that union forfeited to our ghosts. The Eyes of Texas is all of us. As it should have always been. We do not sing at our student-athletes, we sing with them.

The song's message is simple: we uphold a standard that cannot be shirked, even in death. After Gabriel's Horn blows, there is a final reckoning.

Defining that standard is left to us. We decide. Not the people who first performed it 117 years ago. Is there a greater rebuke to that original unveiling than people of every background proudly singing shoulder-to-shoulder, with unity of purpose and clarity of heart, as we have done so many times together? All one, the sons and daughters of Texas. Our living reckoning of a legacy, the resolute exorcism of our ghosts. For at least one moment, all traveling together, in accord with timeless wisdom.

Eight decades past, Mitsubishi, Toshiba, and Kawasaki made the armaments that killed many of our countrymen. Toshiba equipped the men who terrorized Nanking. Mitsubishi engines powered the Zeros that attacked Pearl Harbor. They refined the gasoline poured on American POW's set alight at Palawan. Few Americans bear ill will towards those organizations now. They are the same in name only. They are not the same people, those are not their current ideals, and we are not living in that world.

This is no call for blissful ignorance. We owe it to every member of our Longhorn community to understand and grapple with our history. The noble and the grotesque. We do not lack for either. But we should also be careful about destroying or undermining that which unifies us because it passed through or touched a particular time and place, altered by time's distorting lens cast upon the folkways of a different era.

The Eyes of Texas did not endure because of its disreputable beginning. It endured because it spoke to something deeper. As we grew in understanding, the song grew with us. Because the "us" singing it had changed, too.

"No man ever walks through the same river twice. For it is not the same water and he is not the same man." - Heraclitus

The Eyes of Texas is not the same water.

And we are not the same men.

About the Authors

Paul Wadlington is a Texas graduate and writer/entrepreneur currently living in San Francisco, CA. Paul is the co-founder and managing editor of BarkingCarnival.com and a contributor at Inside Texas. Sign up for the **Thinking Texas Football newsletter** (https://mailchi.mp/5cee48344999/nohoopleheadsallowed) and listen to the Everyone Gets A Trophy podcast with Paul & Kevin on: **Apple**, **Spotify**, **Anchor**

Scott Gerlach is a Texas graduate who stayed in Austin, TX. He works in Human-centered Product Design.

Will Gallagher is a Texas graduate and professional photographer. More of Will's brilliant work can be found at his website http://gallagherstudios.com

Support our sponsor, Gabe Winslow and his mortgage team

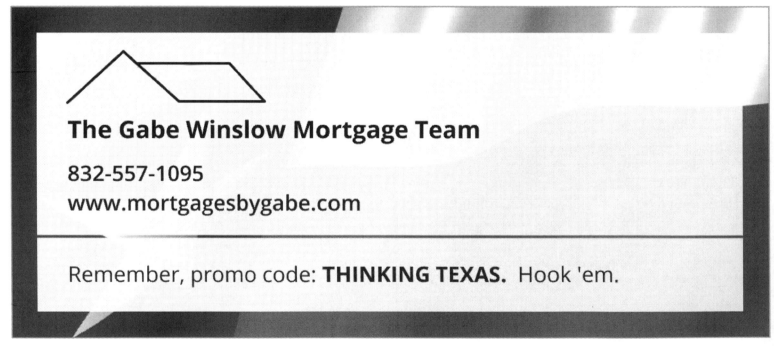

The Gabe Winslow Mortgage Team

832-557-1095

www.mortgagesbygabe.com

Remember, promo code: **THINKING TEXAS.** Hook 'em.

**

If you enjoyed the read, let others know. Your support is vital in allowing us to take the time to create a great product. Thanks for *Thinking Texas Football* with us!

Made in the USA
Coppell, TX
11 July 2022

79819245R10077